Ribs **Foramina** Gladiolus **Lumbar** Manu
c **True Ribs** Xiphoid **Process** Atlas **Axis** C
na Gladiolus **Lumbar** Manubrium **Rib** Ca
iphoid **Process** Atlas Axis **Cervical** Coccy
Lumbar **Manubrium** Rib Cage **Spinal** Col
Atlas Axis **Cervical** Coccyx **False Ribs** Flo
rium **Rib Cage** Spinal **Column** T
rvical **Coccyx** False Ribs Flo F
age Spinal **Column** Sternum **Thoracic** Tru
cyx **False Ribs** Floating **Ribs** Foramina Gl
umn **Sternum** Thoracic **True Ribs** Xipho
Floating **Ribs** Foramina **Gladiolus** Lumb
n **Thoracic** True Ribs Xiphoid **Process** At
Foramina **Gladiolus** Lumbar **Manubriu**
Ribs Xiphoid **Process** Atlas Axis **Cervical**
lus **Lumbar** Manubrium **Rib Cage** Spina
ocess **Atlas** Axis **Cervical** Coccyx **False Ri**
anubrium **Rib Cage** Spinal **Column** Stern
is **Cervical** Coccyx **False Ribs** Floating Ri
Cage Spinal **Column** Sternum **Thoracic** T
cyx **False Ribs** Floating **Ribs** Foramina G
umn **Sternum** Thoracic **True Ribs** Xipho
Floating **Ribs** Foramina **Gladiolus** Lumb
n **Thoracic** True Ribs Xiphoid **Process** At
Foramina **Gladiolus** Lumbar **Manubriu**
Ribs Xiphoid **Process** Atlas Axis **Cervical**
lus **Lumbar** Manubrium **Rib Cage** Spina
ocess **Atlas** Axis **Cervical** Coccyx **False R**

Be Yourself!

Own Yourself!

Know Yourself!

Dr. Bonyfide PRESENTS

For ages 6 to 206!

BONES OF THE RIB CAGE AND SPINE

BOOK 3

A *KNOW YOURSELF, PBC* CREATION
OAKLAND, CALIFORNIA

I am my own muse. I am the subject I know best.

Created by Know Yourself, PBC
Copyright ©2016 Know Yourself, PBC
All rights reserved
www.knowyourself.com

ISBN 978-0-9912968-2-8
Library of Congress Control Number: 2015915707
Printed in China

The subject I want to better.

Frida Kahlo

Acknowledgements from the Team

We would like to thank all of the talented and passionate writers, illustrators, educators, and medical practitioners who participated in the creation of this book. You are all a part of the growing Know Yourself family and we owe you an enormous debt of gratitude for helping us bring this vision to life.

To Nancy "Ella Mental" Howes, our fearless leader, thank you for teaching us that by taking care of ourselves, we take care of everyone around us. To Joanie Thompson, for providing us with a foundation of laughter and hard work.

To the fantastic new members of the Know Yourself team: Kim Baker, Josh Cruickshank, Maiki Interi, Stephanie Mackler, Breena Nuñez, Kimi Owens, Amol Ray, Clint Walker, and Keith "K-Dub" Williams, each of you are key pieces in our quest to help the next generation learn the gifts they already have inside them.

To Derek Bacchus, for your leadership, mentorship, attention to detail, eagerness to help us all refine our crafts, love of books, and for introducing us to the best intern we've ever had, Alexandra.

Enjoy!

Contents

Preface

As a young child and active athlete, I was trying to figure out how to help my body heal fast from various football and other sports injuries. My grandmother took me to my first chiropractic appointment when I was 10 and I still remember the doctor telling me, "Listen to your body — it will tell you what you need to know!" At the time I didn't necessarily know what he meant.

As a chiropractor of 23 years, having had the privilege of treating thousands of patients, I am now very well aware of the importance of knowing your body. An awareness of your body's strengths, limitations, and responses is very powerful, yet not many people actually take the time to learn.

Children have wonderfully curious minds, always yearning and striving to learn. What better subject to learn about than their own body? And what better time to start than while their body is still growing?

The **Know Yourself** book series provides children and the adults who love them with a wonderful tool to learn about themselves in a fun and inspiring way. I am very excited about this book's emphasis on the spine and rib cage, because so many of our bodies' responses and conditions correlate with the spinal cord.

Enjoy the journey and power of learning!

Best Health,

Dr. Matt Rivera
Rivera Chiropractic Group
San Carlos, CA

Dr. Matt Rivera & Family

Welcome!

Want to know your body's secrets?
It's amazing what's inside!
I'll help you learn about yourself.
Hello, I'm Dr. Bonyfide!

Come on a guided tour with me.
Know yourself inside and out.
We'll start with the powerful bones,
as we go along our route.

Your skeleton is a puzzle.
And these parts, they interlock.
But instead of puzzle pieces,
each bone is a building block.

Yes, these bones have names and functions,
for you to learn about.
With discoveries everywhere,
my fun rhymes will help you out.

And before you even know it,
you'll have learned them all with ease.
You'll sing and say the names of bones
just like your ABCs!

Boneology

Osteology* means the study of bones.
It's a word that doctors use.
To make it fun, here's a made-up word—
Boneology* is the word we choose.

"**ology**" at the end of a word
means *the study of*, you see.
And you will learn about your bones.
It's cool to learn **Boneology**!

When you grow up, as it turns out,
you'll have **206** bones in your skeleton.
Osteologists know without a doubt,
boneless, you'd be squishy like gelatin.

Book number 3 explores **51** bones.
They make up your spine and rib cage.
To learn how they work, together and alone,
go ahead and turn the next page.

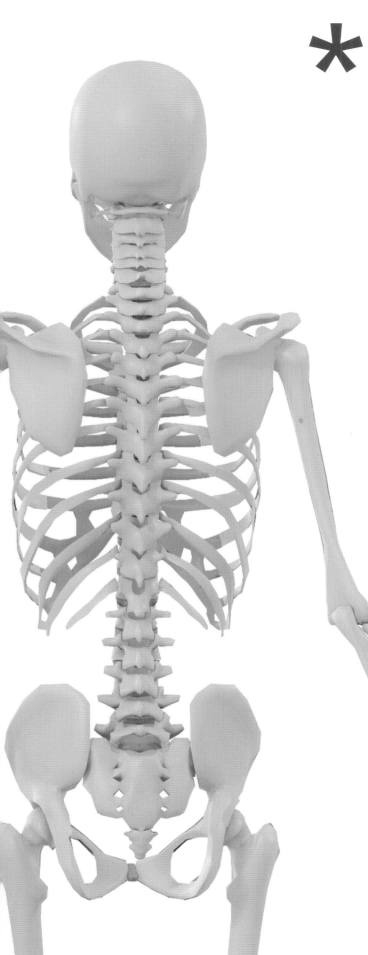

Say them like this:
Osteology **"os-tee-ol-uh-jee"**
Boneology **"bone-ol-uh-jee"**
Osteologists **"os-tee-ol-uh-jists"**

The stressed syllable is always shown in **red**.

How to use our Pronunciation Guide

To help you learn how to pronounce new words, we've invented a fun system. We separate words into syllables, which is something you've probably seen before, but whenever a syllable sounds like a word you might be familiar with, we spell out the actual word. For example, the word spinal would be shown as

"spy-null"

This is a combination of the words "spy" and "null."

Let's start with the big picture.

Touch your back.
Feel the strength within.
There's something hard
underneath your skin.

What is it exactly?
You are feeling your bones—
your living skeletal framework.

Humans are born with approximately
300 bones. As we grow, some bones
fuse together, leaving us with about
206 bones in the adult human body.

What do you think your bones do?

Bones have four main functions:

1. **Movement**: The skeletal system, along with the muscular system, helps people move. This happens because muscles are connected to bones.

2. **Protection**: The skeletal framework protects internal organs like your intestines, bladder, and colon.

3. **Production and Storage**: Marrow found in the bones produces new blood cells to replace aging and damaged ones. Our bones also store extra minerals such as calcium and phosphorus.

4. **Structure**: The 206 bones of your skeletal system give support and shape to your body.

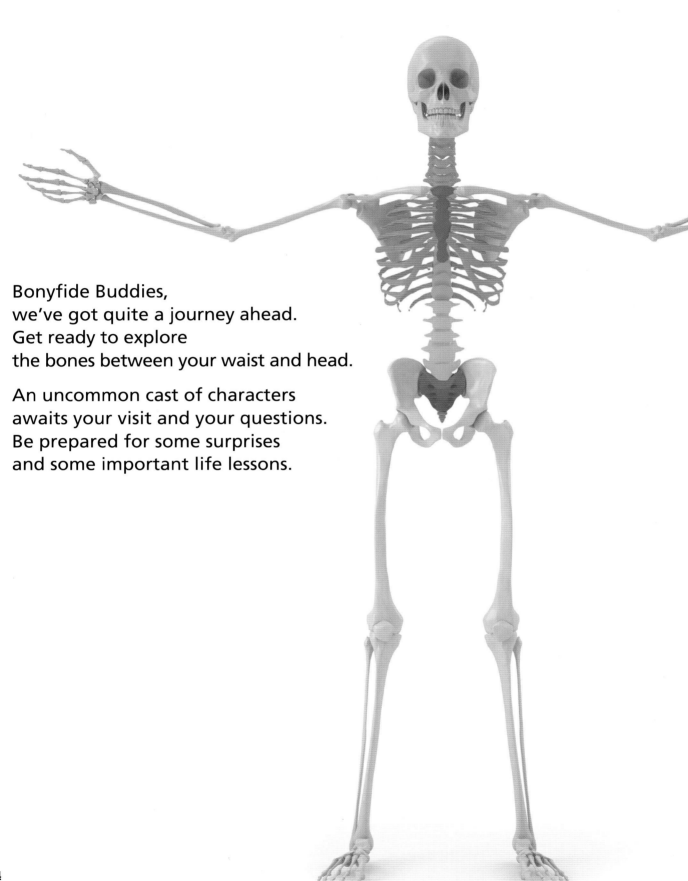

Bonyfide Buddies,
we've got quite a journey ahead.
Get ready to explore
the bones between your waist and head.

An uncommon cast of characters
awaits your visit and your questions.
Be prepared for some surprises
and some important life lessons.

Spine and Rib Cage

You can feel some of your bones,
but you cannot see them.
Put your hands on your hips.
Now move your thumbs in, so they meet at the base of your back.
There, in the center, is where your spine begins.

Touch the center of your chest.
You should feel something like a hard plate.
Did you know there's a bone there,
that helps keep your posture straight?

And connected to that bone are 12 pairs of ribs on each side.
(That's 24 total, explains Dr. Bonyfide.)
They protect your vital organs and sometimes show off your pride.

If you want to know more about what keeps you upright
you've come to the correct place, and we welcome you, with delight!

In this book, you are going to learn the names and locations
of the 51 bones of your **spine** and **rib cage**.

Count them up like this!

   26 bones in the spine
 + **24** bones that span both of your sides
 + **1** bone that keeps them linked tight
 _____
 = **51** bones in the spine and rib cage

Okay, let's explore these bones, starting at the base of your back.

The best

lightning rod

for your protection
is your own spine.

— Ralph Waldo Emerson

11

Spine Overview

The spine is also called the **backbone**.
It has another name, too: **spinal column**.

Say it like this:
"spy-null" — **"call-umm."**

Just like the columns belonging to the great
buildings of ancient Greece and Rome, our
column is one of great strength, and it supports
our body.

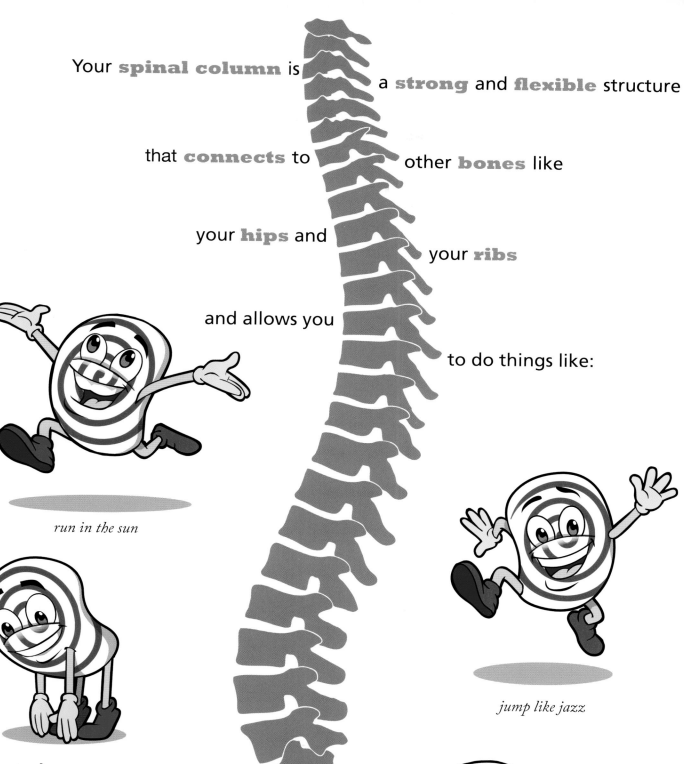

Your **spinal column** is a **strong** and **flexible** structure that **connects** to other **bones** like your **hips** and your **ribs** and allows you to do things like:

run in the sun

touch your toes

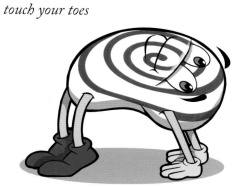

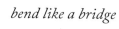

bend like a bridge

jump like jazz

and everything in between! **13**

Our spines can be strong
like a pole or building
COLUMN

but also nimble enough to take

the fluid shape of an ocean wave.

Do All Creatures Have Spines?

Vertebrates are living organisms that have a spine.
Mammals, reptiles, amphibians, birds, and fish
are all vertebrates because they have spines.

Invertebrates are living organisms that don't have a spine.
Jellyfish, sea anemones, spiders, octopuses, and snails
are all invertebrates because they don't have spines.

Activity: Organisms

The word organism comes from the Greek words *organon,* meaning "body organ" and *ismos,* meaning "system."

We say organism to mean "living thing."

Circle the organisms that you think are vertebrates.

The whole spine might feel like
one really loooong bone,
but it is made up of **26 bones**
called **vertebrae**
that are stacked
on top of one another.

Say it like this:
"**ver-tuh-bray**."

Your spine extends from your neck,
just below your earlobes, all the way
down to the very bottom of your back.
This area is known as your buttocks,
also called your butt, for short.

The spine houses the **spinal cord**,
which is the bundle of nerve fibers
and tissue that carries messages
between the brain and the rest of
the body.

Watching your
own back is a sign
of flexibility.

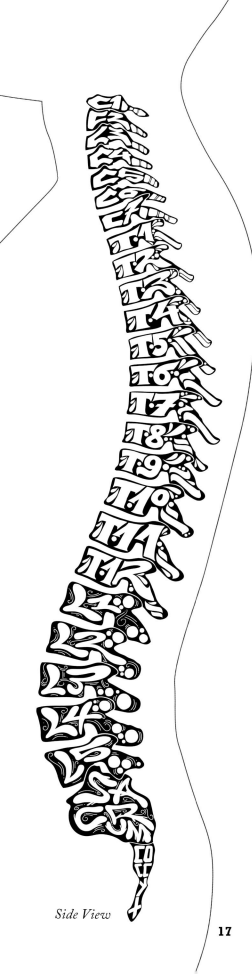

Side View

17

Spine Sections

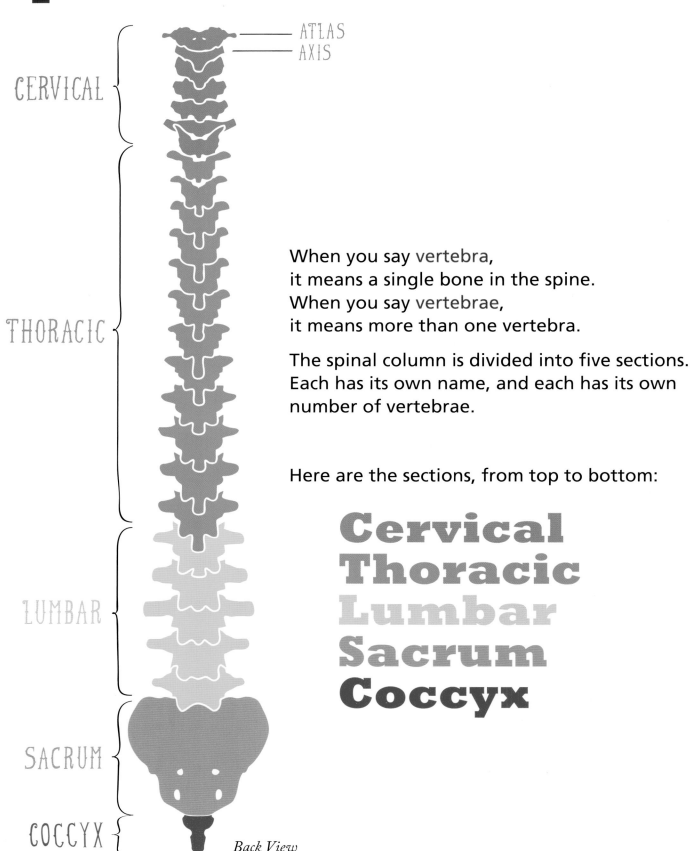

CERVICAL

— ATLAS
— AXIS

THORACIC

LUMBAR

SACRUM

COCCYX

Back View

When you say vertebra,
it means a single bone in the spine.
When you say vertebrae,
it means more than one vertebra.

The spinal column is divided into five sections.
Each has its own name, and each has its own
number of vertebrae.

Here are the sections, from top to bottom:

Cervical
Thoracic
Lumbar
Sacrum
Coccyx

The **Cervical 7** keeps your neck in check.

The **Thoracic 12** owns the most back bones.

The **Lumbar 5** lets your lower back thrive.

The **Sacrum** and the **Coccyx** are hard to speak,

but one is shaped like an anchor

and the other like a beak.

Activity: Spine Search

Sit in a chair with your feet flat on the floor. Gently bend forward until your chest touches your thighs, and try to touch your toes. With one arm, reach behind yourself and see if you can feel any bony bumps in the middle of your back.

Do you feel them?

Those are your vertebrae.

Coccyx

Say it like this:
"kok-siks."

Isn't this the coccyx?! That's the part of the spine Hollie injured!

That's right, Pinky. The coccyx is the ground floor of *this* building.

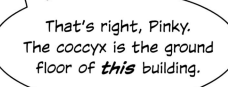

The coccyx rests
at the base of the spine,
and it helps us balance
when sitting.

It's shaped like a beak
and is very unique,
so its name
is really quite fitting.

While you might not be able to feel it,
the coccyx is the lowest
bone in your spine.

It is also known as the tailbone.

Coccyx comes from the Greek word *kokkux,*
or cuckoo—a type of bird—and the end of
the tailbone is said to look like a bird's beak.

So the coccyx provides stability, support, and balance.

At birth our coccyx has three to five soft, separate bones, but as we get older, those bones harden and fuse together.

This process is known as ossification.

Say it like this:
"**aw-sih-fuh-kay-shun**."

Ossi-what?

Ossification is an important process of bone growth that takes place throughout our bodies. By the time we are adults, our coccyx turns into one hard bone.

Newborn   *Child*   *Adult*

Activity: Coccyx Quiz

List three facts that you have learned about the coccyx.

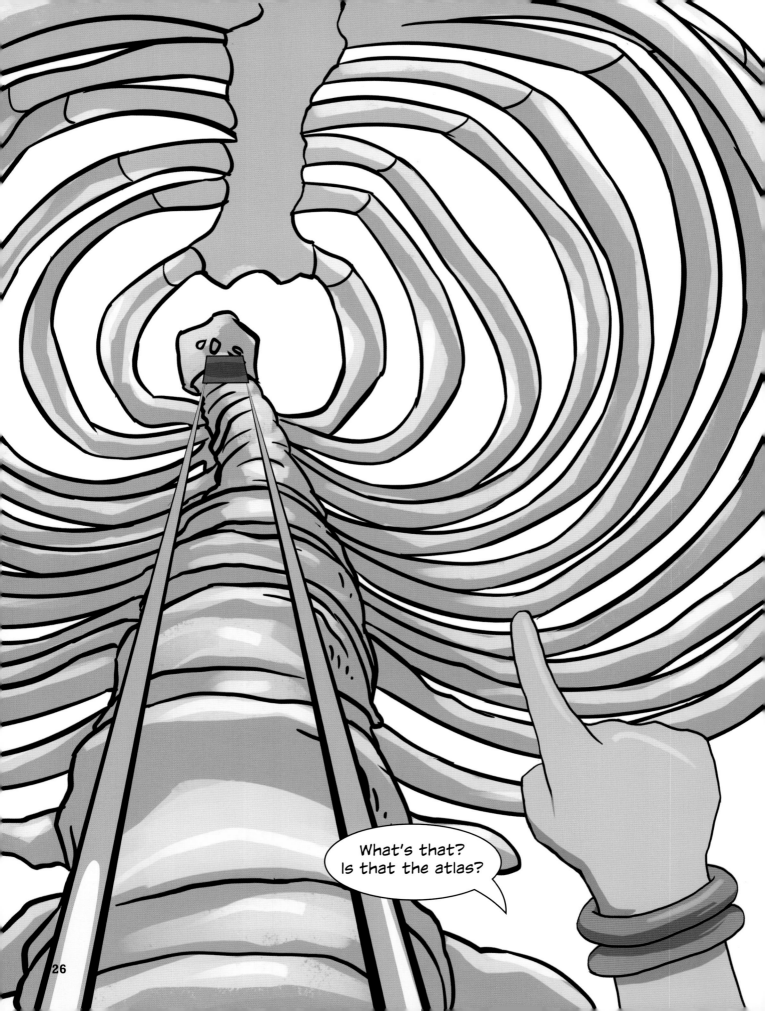

Letters to Vinny

Dear Mr. Vertebrae:

When I was skateboarding I fell down and landed on my tailbone.

It REALLY hurt.

Why did it hurt so bad?

Signed,

Hollie

Dear Hollie:

Just like the muscles in your body, bones can get bruised too! But have no fear, because bone bruises heal over time. It may hurt to walk or sit for a couple weeks, so you might just have to give up the skateboard and watch some cat videos instead!

Heal well,

Vinny V.

Sacrum

Up and up we go,

Traveling through the spine,

Heading to the sacrum,

On Vinny's elevator line!

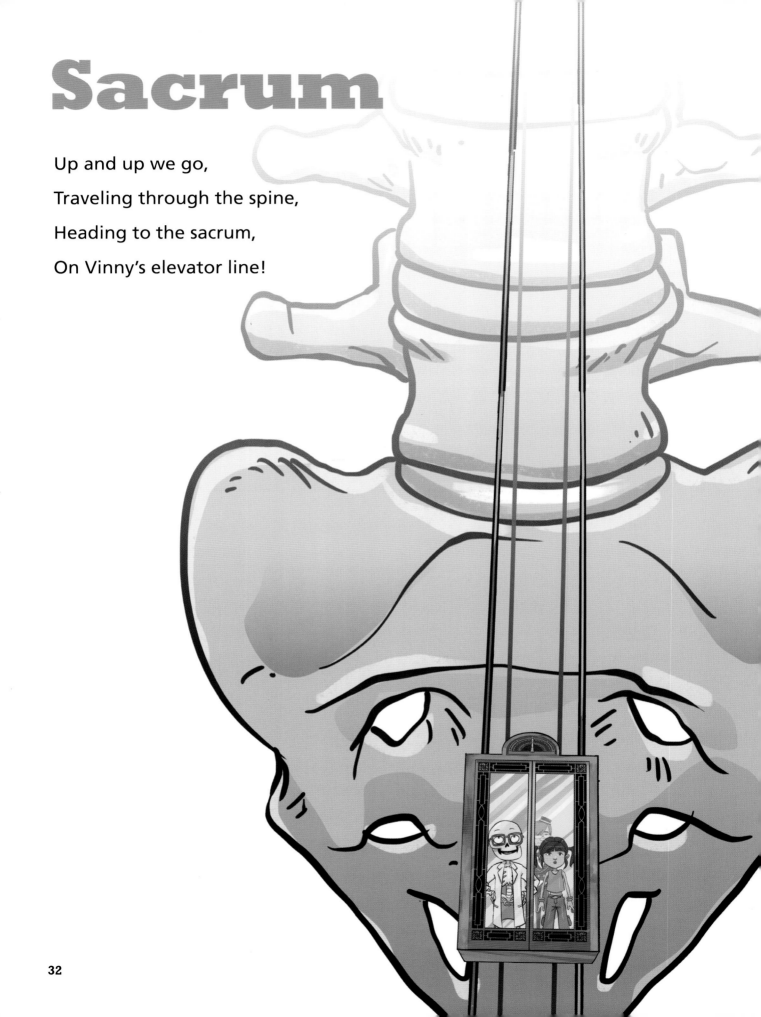

Now Arriving... Floor "S" Sacrum

Say it like this:
"say-crum."

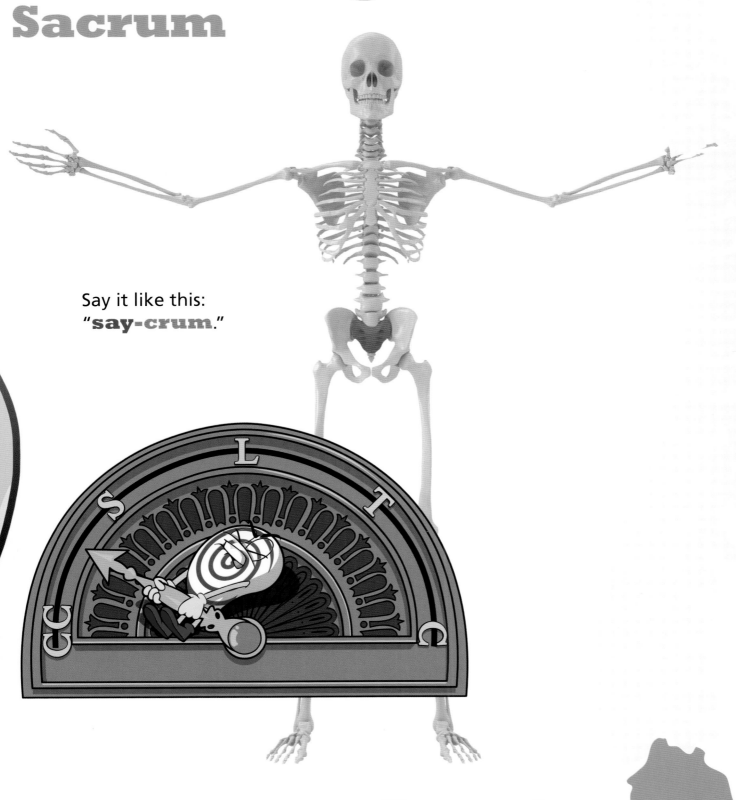

You are here.

The bottom of the sacrum is connected to the top of the coccyx. The top of the sacrum is connected to the lumbar section.

The sacrum forms the posterior, or backside, of the pelvis. The sacrum, along with the hips, helps to support the body's weight.

Etymology

Say it like this:
"**et-a-mol-a-jee**."

The etymology of a word
is how it began.
Some are quite funny,
some are quite bland.

Sacrum comes from the Latin word *os sacrum,*
meaning "sacred bone."

Previously, the bone was called the holy bone,
because of an ancient belief
that this bone was indestructible.

Activity: Verte-Break

Poses like these can help to strengthen our sacrum and other bones. Give them a shot.

Sacrum: Foramina

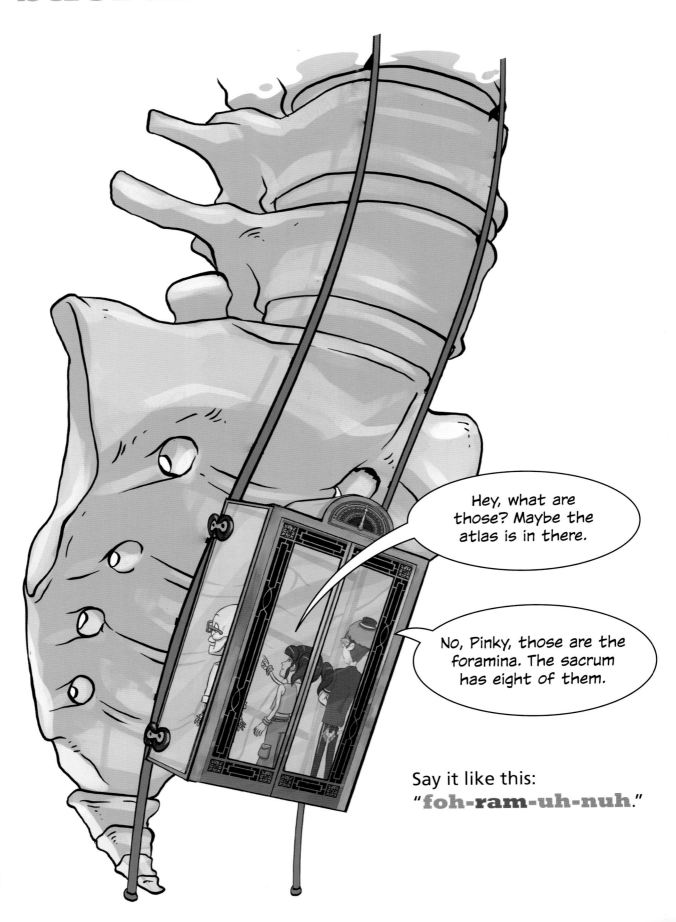

Hey, what are those? Maybe the atlas is in there.

No, Pinky, those are the foramina. The sacrum has eight of them.

Say it like this:
"foh-ram-uh-nuh."

Foramina are holes that line both sides of the sacrum. These openings are for nerves to travel through. This is why the sacrum might be called the most "hole-y" bone in the spine!

The sacrum is like an anchor in our spine that connects our upper body to our lower body.

Activity: Colors of the Spine

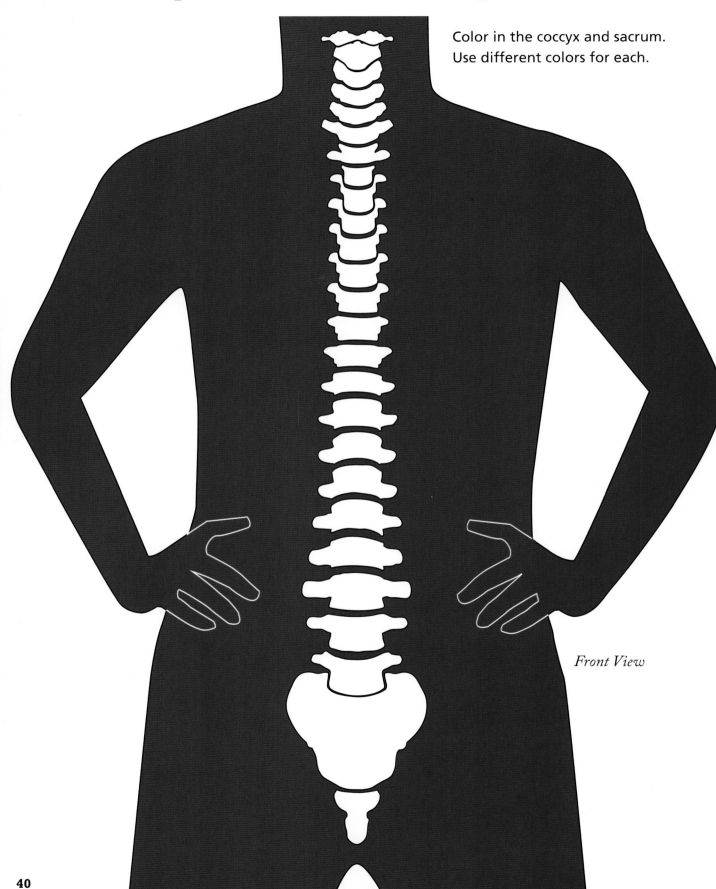

Color in the coccyx and sacrum. Use different colors for each.

Front View

Letters to Vinny

Hey Vin,
Why do kids have more bones than adults?

Signed,
Tony Bonez

Dear Tony,

When you were born, you probably had five vertebrae in your sacrum and four vertebrae in your coccyx, but by the time you are an adult, those once-soft bones will have hardened, or ossified, to become one large, protective bone at the base of your back—almost like a shield for the bottom of your spine! So that is why most kids have 33 bones in their spines, but most adults have 26.

Sincerely,
Vinny V.

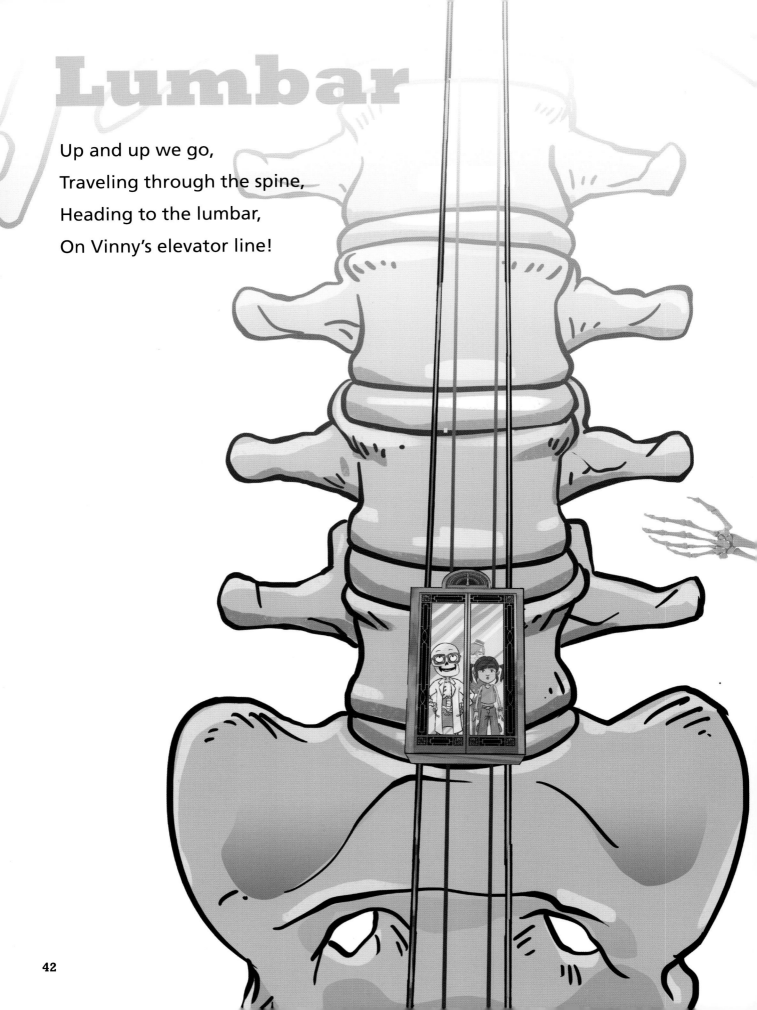

Lumbar

Up and up we go,
Traveling through the spine,
Heading to the lumbar,
On Vinny's elevator line!

Now Arriving... Floor "L" Lumbar

Say it like this: **"lum-bar."**

You are here.

The lumbar is the strongest of your spine's five sections.

The five vertebrae in the lumbar section are thick and sturdy to help support the weight of your body. They are important in movements like twisting, bending, and especially lifting.

There are five different bones in the lumbar section of the spine. They are called L1, L2, L3, L4, and L5.

The L5 vertebra is on the bottom. L5 bears more body weight than any of the other 23 vertebrae that sit atop it in the spinal column. This is why L5 is the largest and strongest vertebra in the lumbar section. Got it?

THIS BRACE WILL DO **WONDERS** FOR YOUR BACK.

NOW, I'M SURE TO STRETCH MY LOWER BACK BEFORE LIFTING ANYTHING MORE THAN A FEW POUNDS.

SO, THANKS TO VINNY VERTEBRAE, I'VE BEEN ABLE TO MAINTAIN A STRONG SPINE.

BUT HONESTLY, IT'S IMPORTANT TO TAKE CARE OF YOUR LUMBAR WHEN YOU'RE YOUNG, SO THAT IT DOESN'T ACT UP ON YOU WHEN YOU GET OLDER.

Activity: Colors of the Spine

Color in the lumbar section.

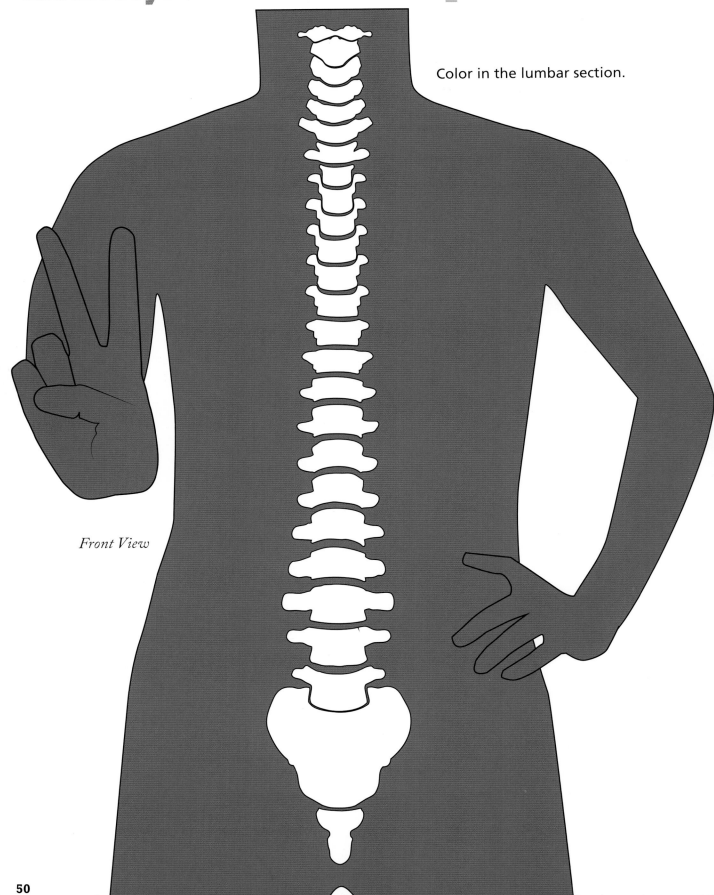

Front View

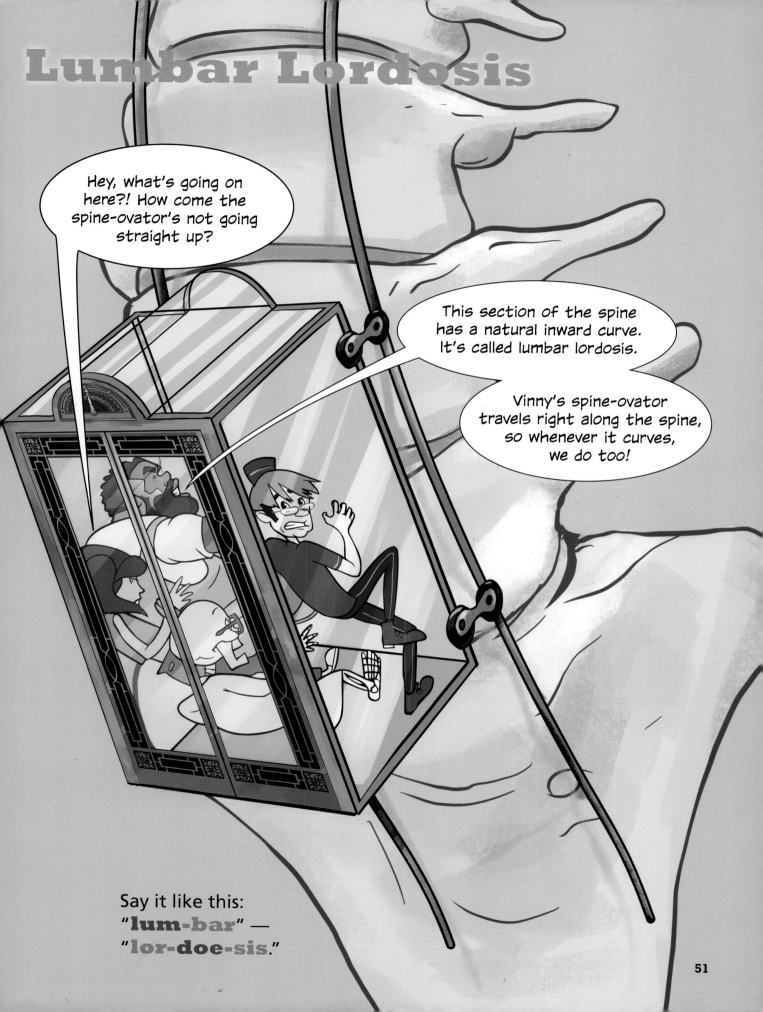

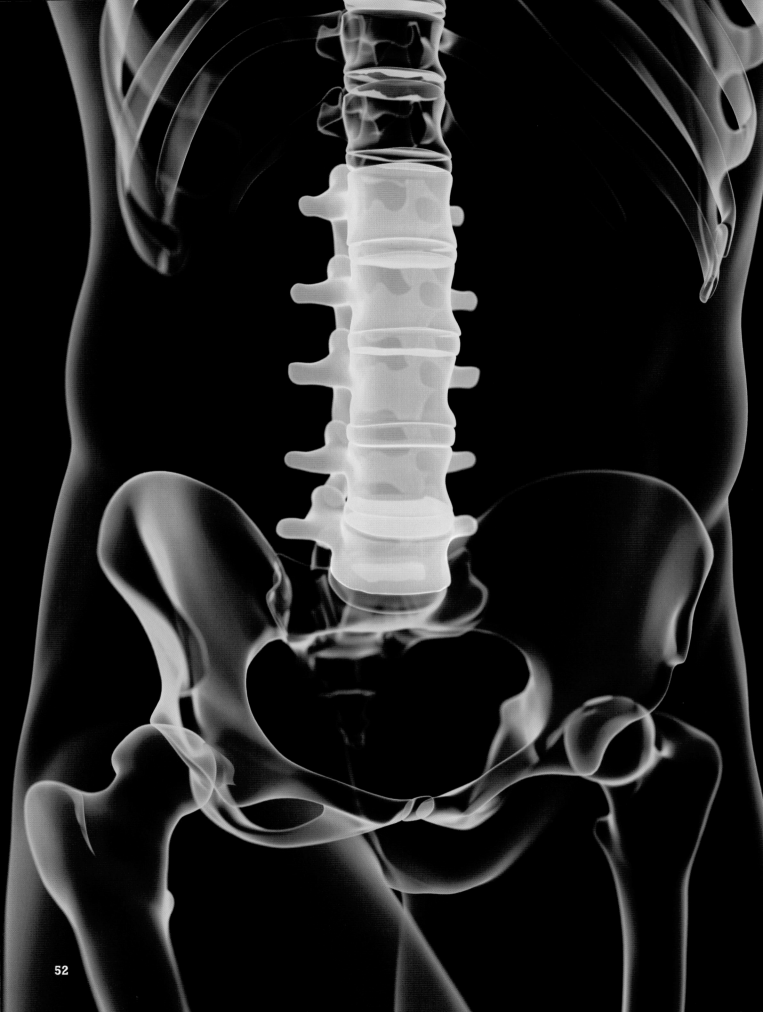

Now that you've gotten a sense of the entire lumbar section, let's take a look at an individual vertebra. Here's how L3 looks from multiple angles.

Side

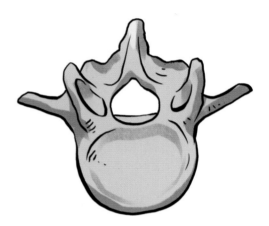

Top

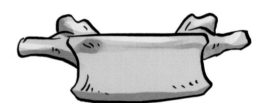

Front

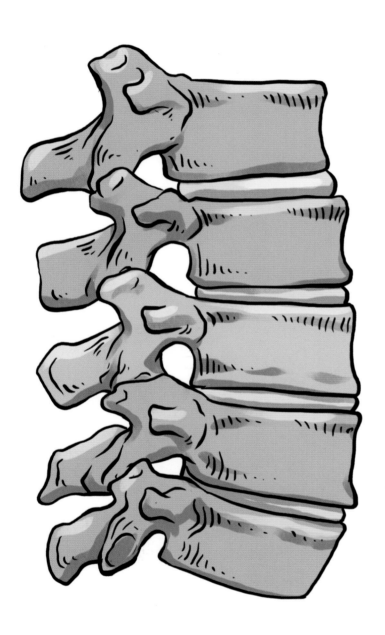

Side View

Back

Letters to Vinny

Dear Vertebrae Expert,

I recently injured my lumbar section when I bent down to pick up an old bookshelf. Once I recover, how can I make sure not to hurt my lower back again?

Sincerely,
Oliver Twisted

Hi there Oliver!

One thing you should always do before picking up anything heavy is take a moment to stretch out your back. Then, make sure to bend your knees down, and keep your back straight, so you're not straining your lumbar section by leaning forward to pick things up...

Your Pal,
Lumbar Jack

Activity: Stretch it Out

Extension

Here are a few stretches you can do to loosen up the lumbar section, especially before you lift anything heavy.

Flexion

Extension ("ek-**sten**-shun") is when your spine lengthens and your chest moves outward.

Flexion ("**flek**-shun") is when your spine bends, like when you bend over to touch your toes.

Lateral Flexion ("**ladder**-ull" — "**flek**-shun") is when your spine stretches while you tilt from side to side.

Now it's your turn!
Give each of these movements a try.

Lateral Flexion

Activity: Verte-Break

That does it for this floor, friends.

Before we leave here, let's review the shapes of the bones we've seen so far.
Draw each of the bones below:

Coccyx   (one bone)   (hint: bird's beak)
Sacrum   (one bone)   (hint: anchor)
Lumbar   (five bones)   (hint: do you really need one?)

Thoracic

Up and up we go,

Traveling through the spine,

Heading to the thoracic,

On Vinny's elevator line!

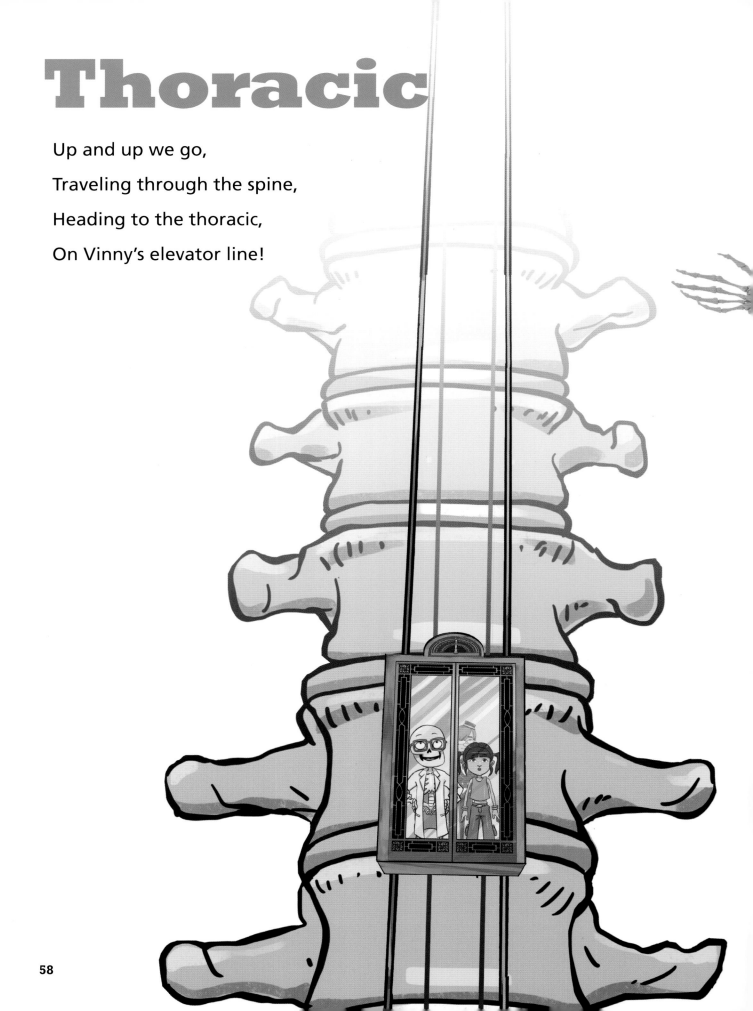

Now Arriving... Floor "T"
Thoracic

Say it like this:
"thor-ra-sick."

You are here.

60

The thoracic section begins just below your shoulders, and extends down the middle of your back. It helps me give great hugs.

Come on in for a group hug, buddies!

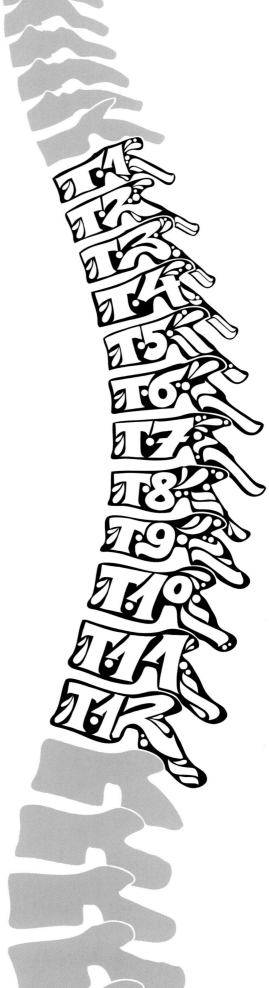

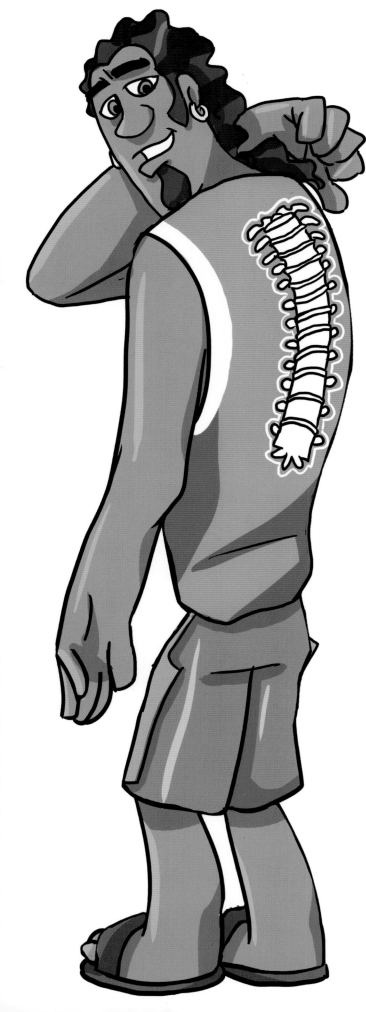

Now that I've made myself comfortable, let's take a look at the thoracic section. You can see it right here on the back of my shirt. This is the longest section in the spine. It makes up the middle and upper part of the back.

The thoracic section has 12 vertebrae. They are called T1 to T12.

The thoracic section has more than twice as many vertebrae as the lumbar section.

Thoracic Kyphosis

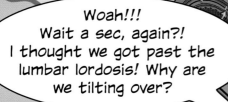

Woah!!!
Wait a sec, again?!
I thought we got past the lumbar lordosis! Why are we tilting over?

Ah, I see you've already learned about the spine's curving ways. Well, here on Floor T, we have another natural curve. This one is an outward curve. It's called thoracic kyphosis.

Say it like this:
"thor-ra-sick" —
"ky-foe-sis."

Kyphosis comes from the Greek
word *kuphosis,* which means

"bent" and "hunchbacked."

Rib Tickler *Q: Where did the Egyptian mummy go to get her back fixed?*
A: The Cairo…practor.

Activity: Colors of the Spine

Color in the thoracic section.

Front View

69

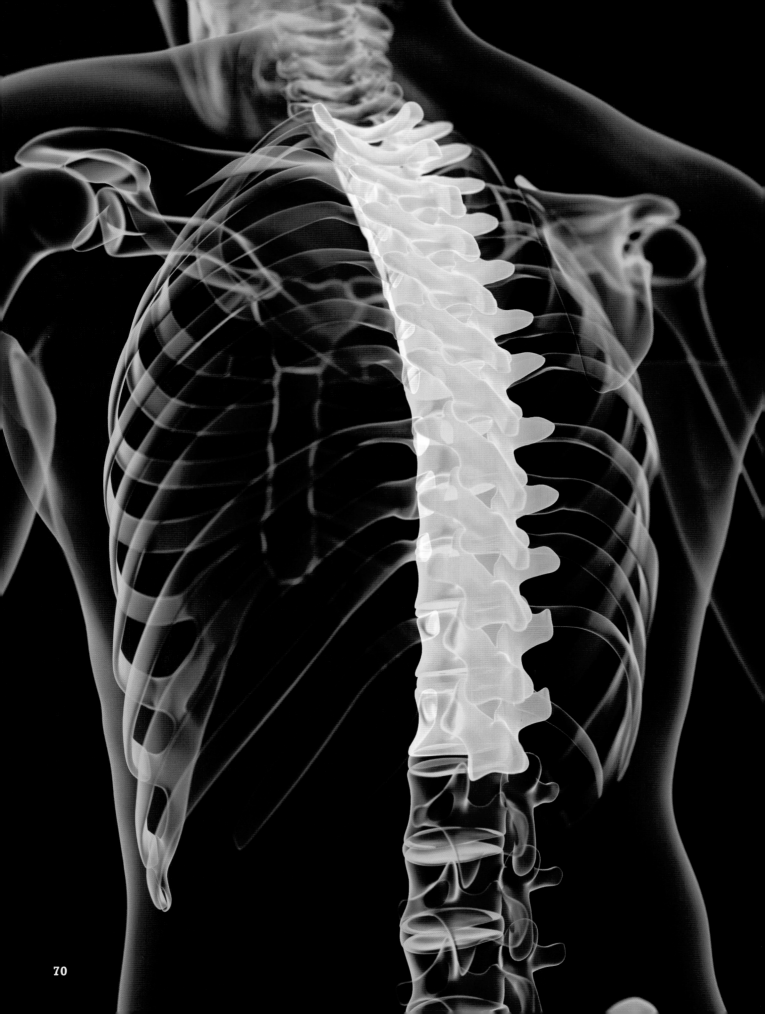

Now that you've gotten a sense of the entire thoracic section, let's take a look at an individual vertebra. Here's how T6 looks from multiple angles.

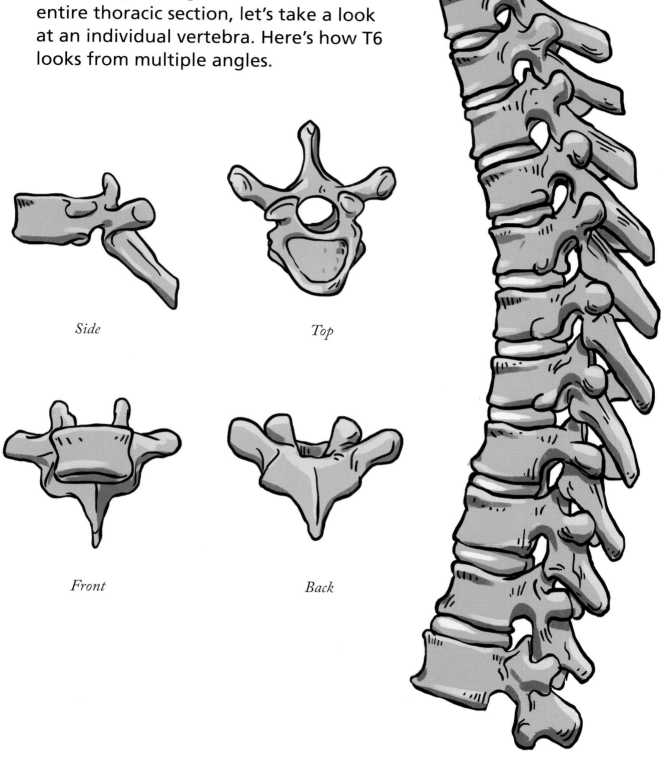

Side

Top

Front

Back

Side View

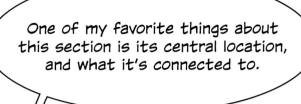

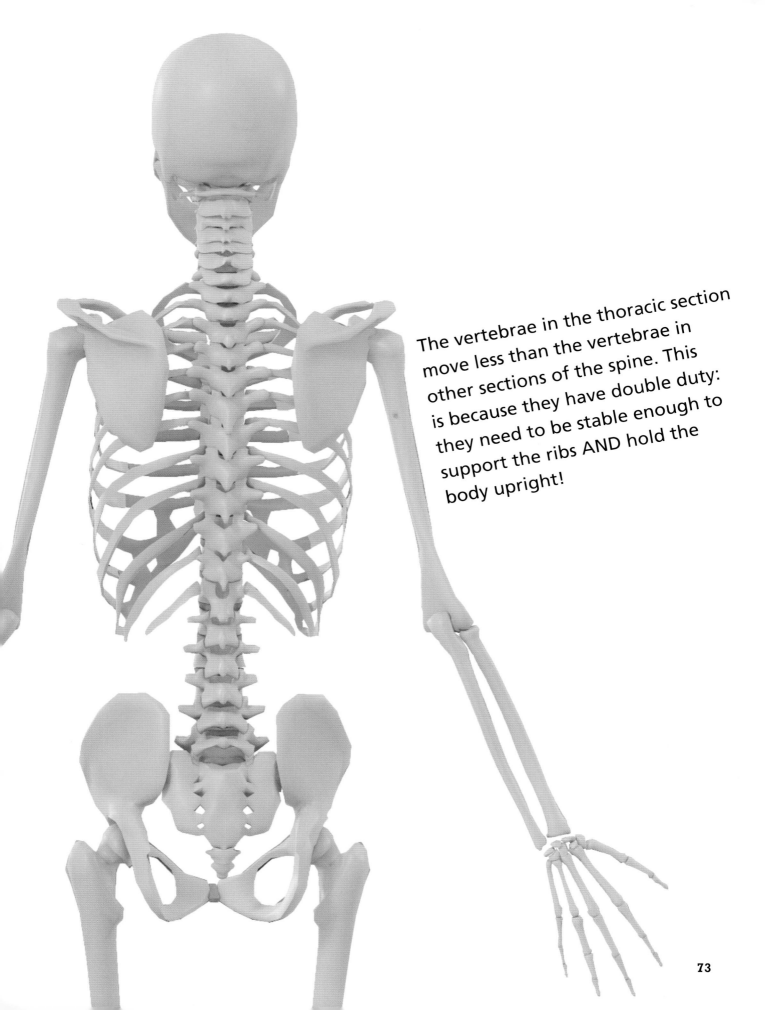

The vertebrae in the thoracic section move less than the vertebrae in other sections of the spine. This is because they have double duty: they need to be stable enough to support the ribs AND hold the body upright!

Activity: Rib Wrap

Everybody do the rib wrap!
Reach for your thoracic to feel fantastic!

Rib Tickler *Q: What kind of newspaper article did the chiropractor write?*
A: A spinal column.

Letters to Vinny

Mister Vinny,

The word thoracic sounds funny.
Where does it come from?

Sincerely,
Bounski

Thoracic comes from the Greek word *thorax,* meaning "middle-section." A thorax, or mid-section, can also be found in other cuddly creatures like bees, ants, and butterflies.

thorax

A healthy outside

starts from the inside.

— Robert Urich

Now Detouring...

Up and up we…

Urr, wait a minute…

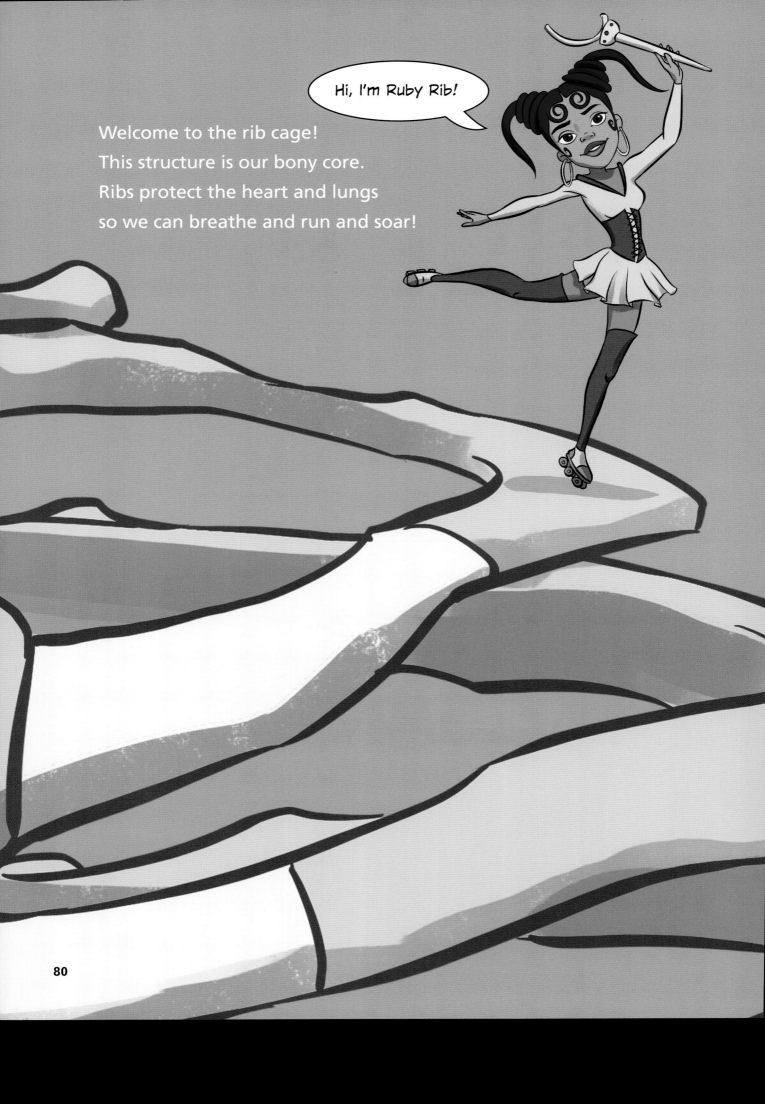

Welcome to the rib cage!
This structure is our bony core.
Ribs protect the heart and lungs
so we can breathe and run and soar!

80

Rib Cage Overview

The rib cage is made up of three different parts: ribs, sternum, and vertebrae.

The ribs are the 12 pairs of arched bones that form the skeletal structure of your chest. (Remember, that's 24 in total.)

The sternum is a long, sword-shaped bone located in the center of your chest, along the midline of your body.

And, as you just learned, 12 vertebrae make up the thoracic section of your spine.

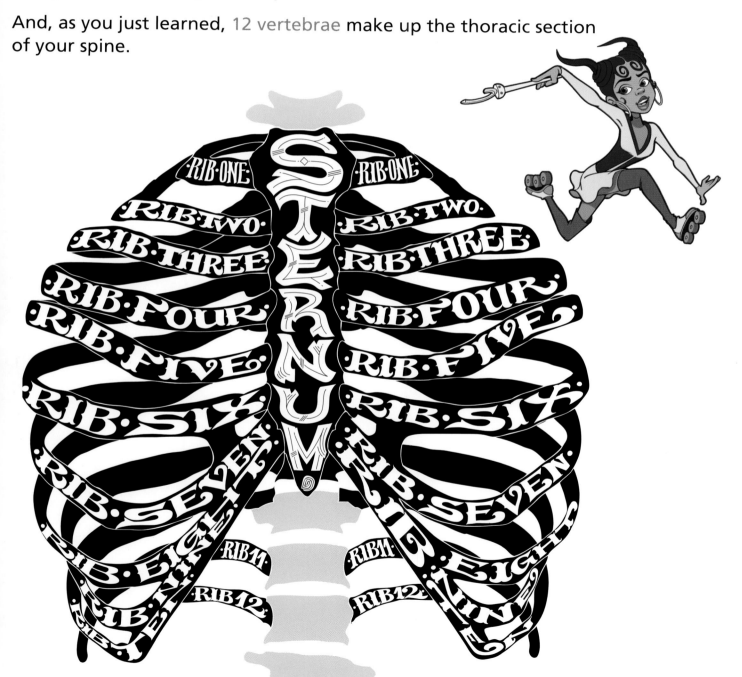

83

Rib Cage: Ribs

There are 12 pairs of ribs, which are numbered 1 to 12, from top to bottom.

All ribs connect to a corresponding thoracic vertebra in the spine (for example, rib 1 connects to T1, rib 2 connects to T2, and so on).

Cartilage connects the ribs to the sternum.

Cartilage is a strong but flexible material found in some parts of the body.
It provides support without being as hard or rigid as bone.
Because it's so flexible, it helps the rib cage expand.

Say it like this:
"car-ta-lidj."

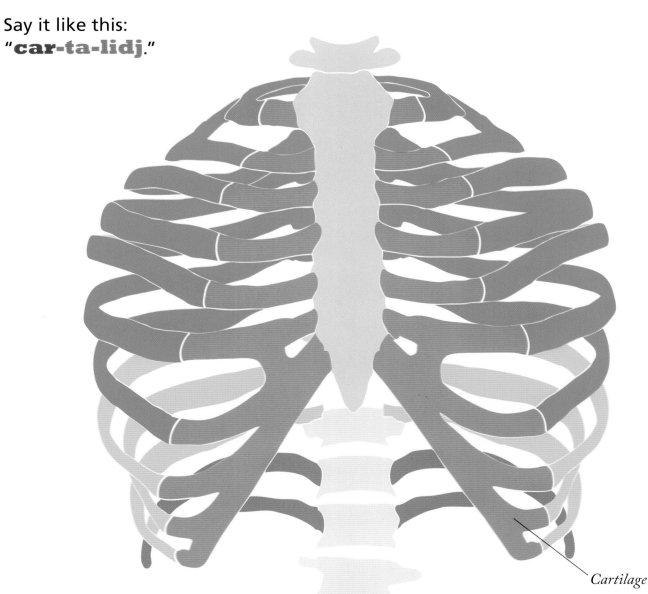

Cartilage

84

Having 12 pairs of ribs
is no laughing matter.

From the first to the last,
their shape is curved and then flatter.

For every one on the right,
there is a match on the left.

Which makes for a strong
and supple bony life-vest.

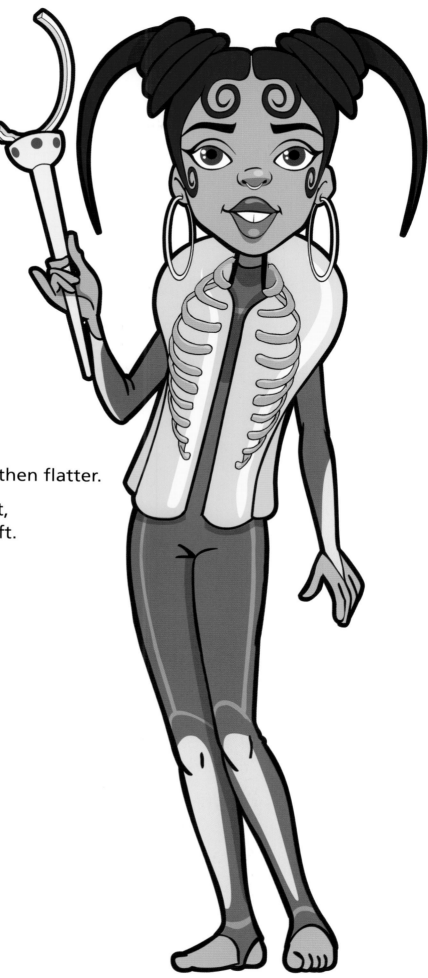

Ribs: True Ribs

The ribs are separated into three different groups: true ribs, false ribs, and floating ribs.

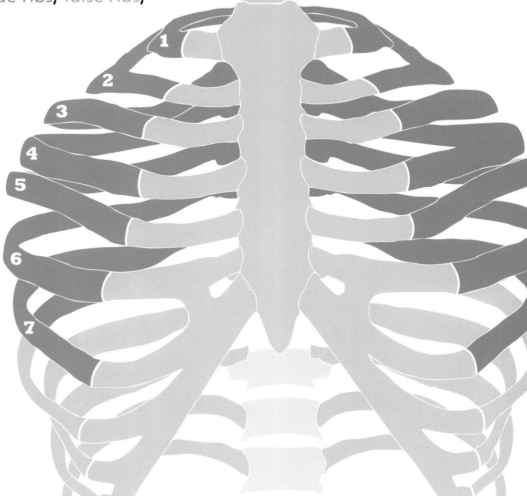

Ribs 1 through 7 are called true ribs.

The true ribs start just beneath the collar bone and end all the way down in the middle of the torso.

They are called true ribs because they connect directly to the sternum by a single strip of cartilage.

Ribs 1 through 7 all have their own strip of cartilage that connects them to the sternum.

Ribs: False Ribs

Ribs 8, 9, and 10 are called false ribs because they don't connect to the sternum with their own strip of cartilage.

They reach up and attach to the cartilage of rib 7.

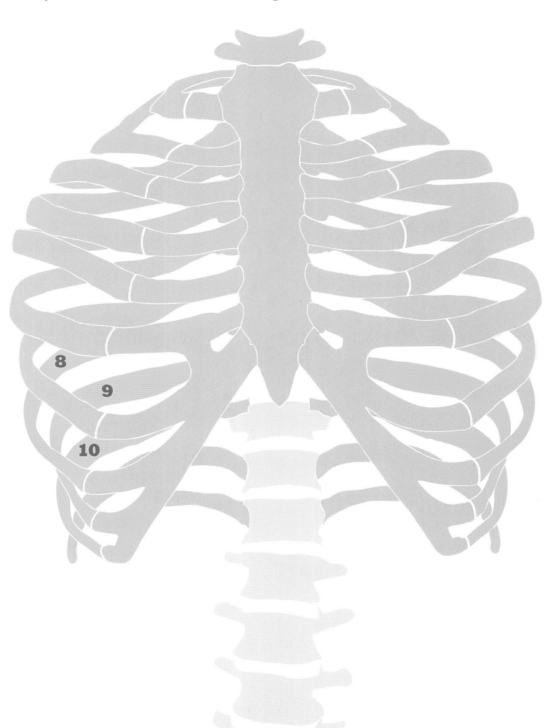

Ribs: Floating Ribs

Ribs 11 and 12 are called floating ribs because they don't attach to the sternum or to cartilage.

They start at the 11th and 12th thoracic vertebrae and simply end in the middle of our bodies, just above the outside of our hip bones. Floating ribs are thus smaller than the true ribs and the false ribs.

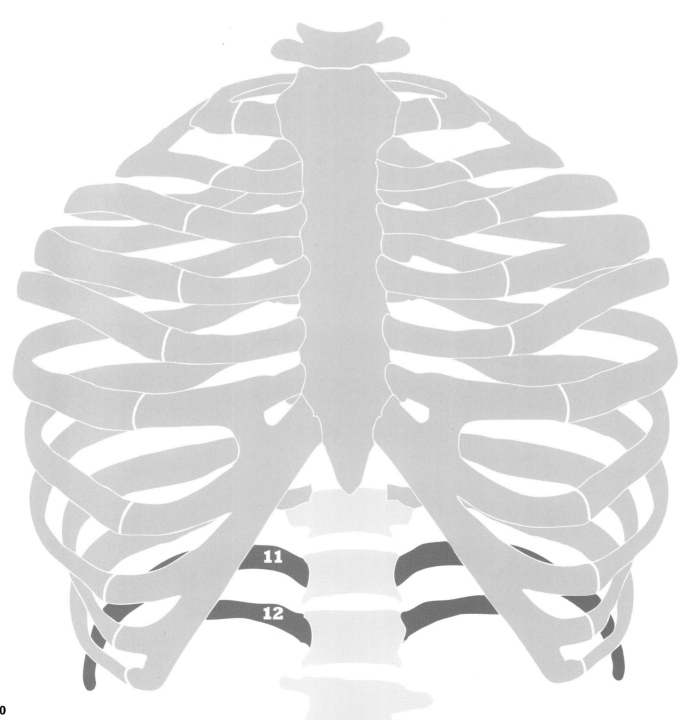

Activity: Rib Recap

1. Name the three different parts that make up the rib cage.

2. How many pairs of ribs does the human body contain?

3. What are the names of the three different types of ribs?

4. Name one of the main functions of the ribs.

5. Which vertebra does rib 7 connect to?

6. What is cartilage?

7. There are ___ pairs of true ribs.

[5 * 7 * 14]

8. There are ___ pairs of false ribs.

[2 * 3 * 6]

9. There are ___ pairs of floating ribs.

[2 * 3 * 6]

Activity: Verte-Break

Now that you've learned about all the ribs, how about trying to locate them in your own body?

Raise up your arm.

Place your fingers on your armpit. Apply a little pressure.

Now start slowly sliding your hand down your side, counting each bump you feel along the ride.

How many ribs did you find?

Rib Tickler *Q: What did the two-ribbed frog say to the snake with 200 ribs?*

A: Hey friend! I could use a spare rib!

Rib Tickler *In 16th Century Germany and England (where the word* ribbe *first shows up) people used the word to mean "joke" or "tease." They made the connection that when you tickle someone in the rib they do the same thing as when you tell them a joke. They laugh!*

93

Activity: **Colors of the Ribs**

Color in the three types of ribs, using one color for true ribs, another color for false ribs, and another color for floating ribs.

Say their names out loud as you color them.

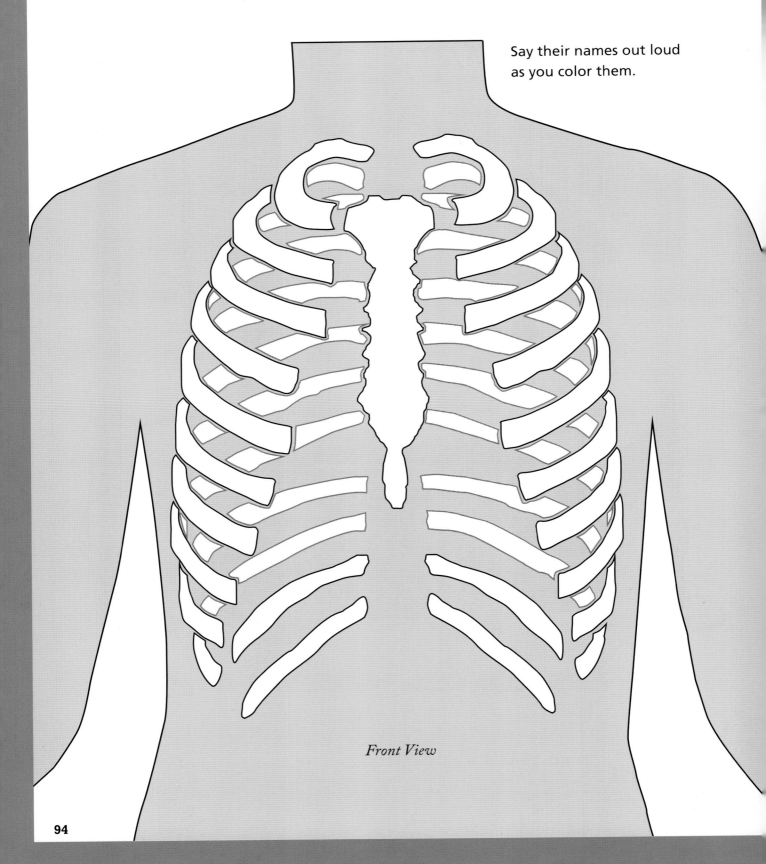

Front View

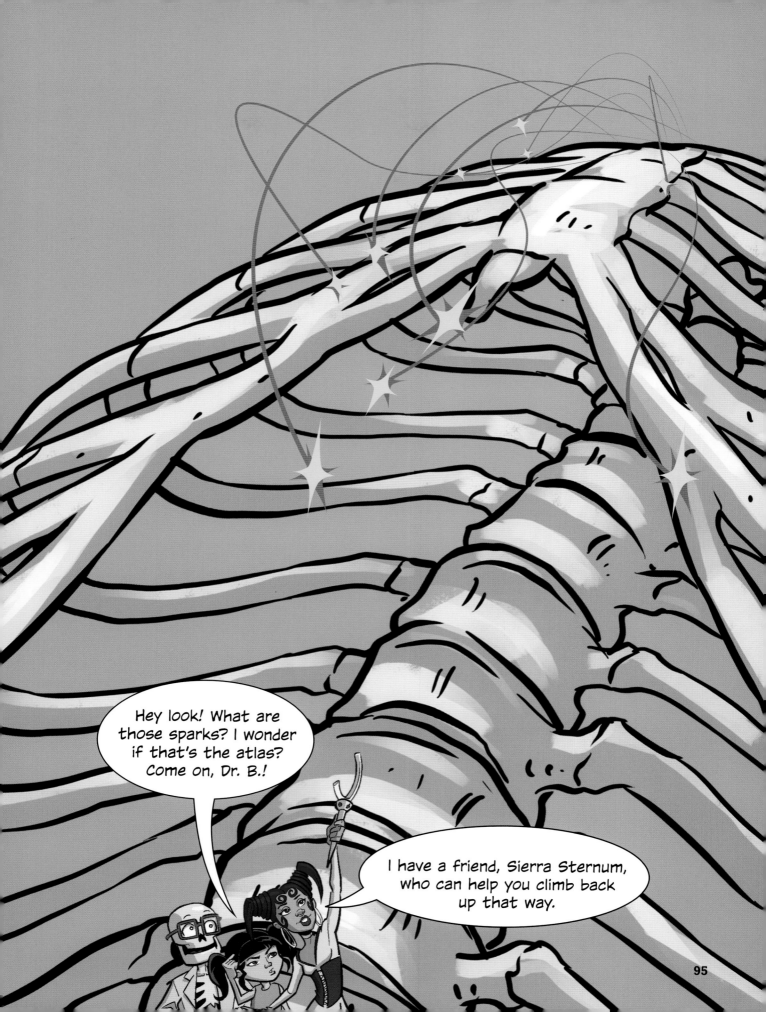

Rib Cage:
Sternum

The sternum is flat and protects the front of the body.
Its job is to stabilize the rib cage and protect the heart and arteries of the chest.

Say it like this: **"stir-num."**

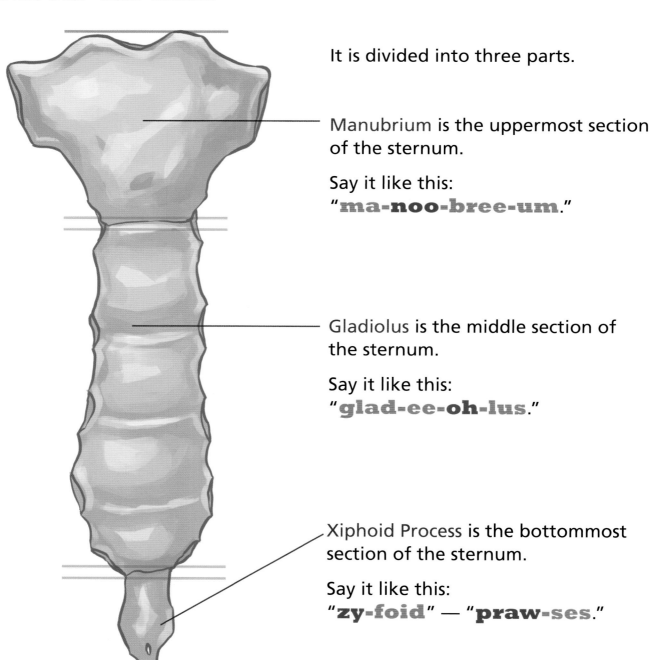

It is divided into three parts.

Manubrium is the uppermost section of the sternum.

Say it like this:
"ma-noo-bree-um."

Gladiolus is the middle section of the sternum.

Say it like this:
"glad-ee-oh-lus."

Xiphoid Process is the bottommost section of the sternum.

Say it like this:
"zy-foid" — **"praw-ses."**

In Latin, the language of the Romans, each of the sternum's three sections matches a section on my sword.

Manubrium means "handle."

Gladiolus means "little sword."

Xiphoid means "shaped like a sword."

It also comes in handy when I'm rock-climbing and need to cut through branches or bushes.

BACK STORY: Sierra Sternum

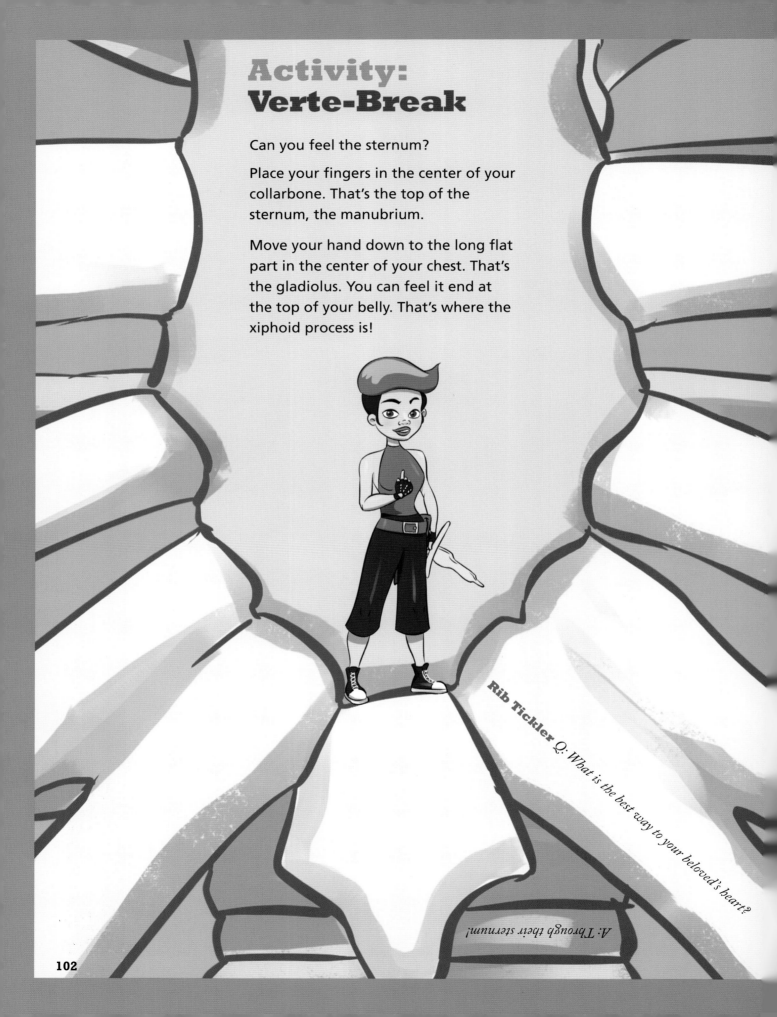

Activity: Verte-Break

Can you feel the sternum?

Place your fingers in the center of your collarbone. That's the top of the sternum, the manubrium.

Move your hand down to the long flat part in the center of your chest. That's the gladiolus. You can feel it end at the top of your belly. That's where the xiphoid process is!

Rib Tickler Q: What is the best way to your beloved's heart?

A: Through their sternum!

Xiphoid Process

The xiphoid process is a soft,
pointy piece of cartilage.
It takes up to 40 years before it
hardens completely into bone!

Baby Xiphoid

Middle Xiphoid

Elder Xiphoid

I want to be
a xiphoid when
I grow up!

Activity: Colors of the Sternum

Color in the three parts of the sternum, using one color
for the manubrium, another color for the gladiolus,
and another color for the xiphoid process.

Say their names out loud
as you color them.

Front View

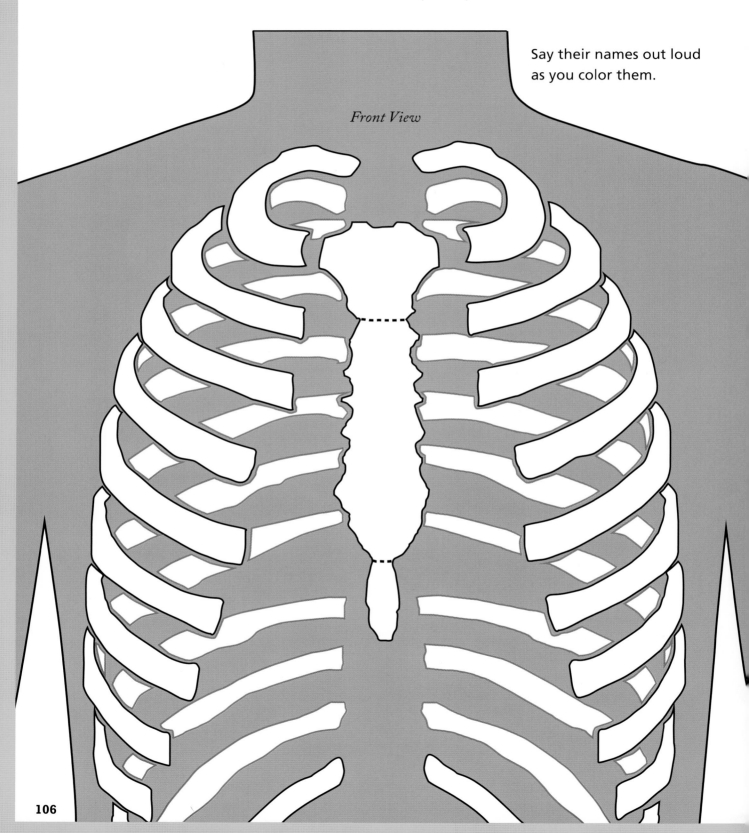

Letters to Vinny

Dearest Vincent:

I was finishing up at the skate park yesterday when another skater stepped in front of me. Before I could gather myself and stop, I slammed right into her, chest first. We both stumbled to the ground, and had sore ribs afterwards. When I told my mom, she said, "Better be glad you had those ribs to keep you from having a sore lung or heart!" What did she mean?

Yours truly,
Super Sore Skater

Hey Soreski!

Your mom is on point! She knows that the ribs protect you from really hurting yourself when you run or skate! If not for your ribs, that collision could have bruised your lungs, and that would really make you catch your breath!

You need to be careful when skating. Sometimes it can take several months to heal from a skateboarding injury. In fact, I heard that just happened to a young skater.

Get strong soon!
Vinny V.

Fall down
seven times
get up
eight.

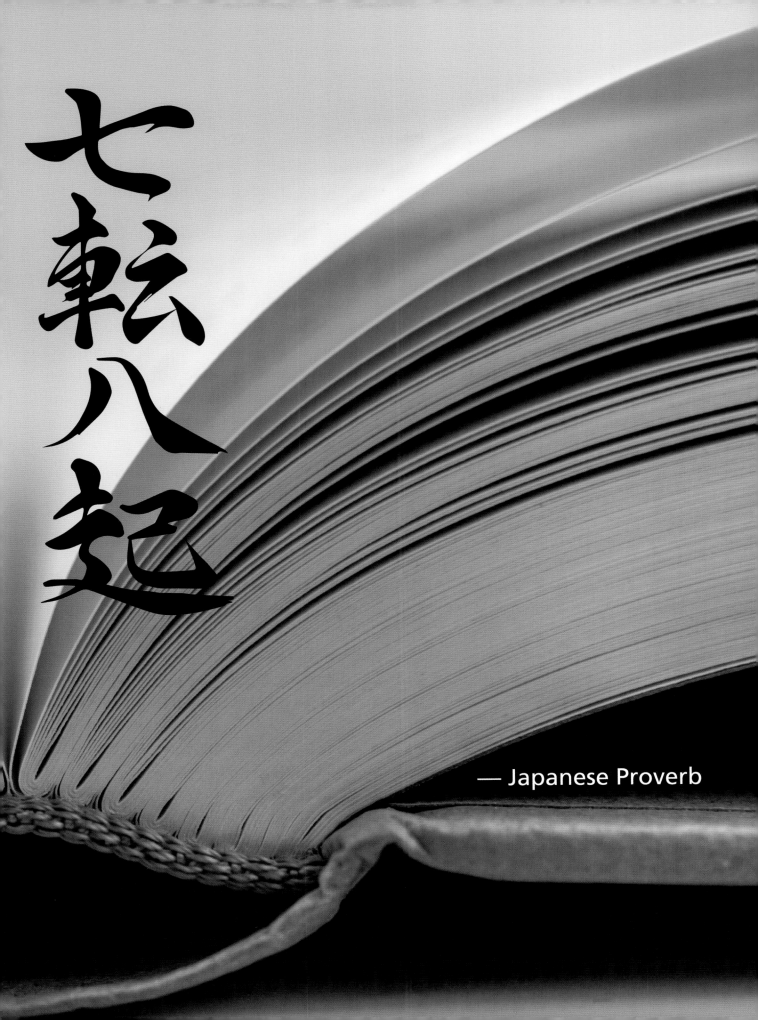

七転八起

— Japanese Proverb

Cervical

Up and up we go,
Traveling through the spine,
Heading to the cervical,
On Vinny's elevator line!

Now Arriving... Floor "C"
Cervical

You are here.

Say it like this:
"sir-vuh-cul."

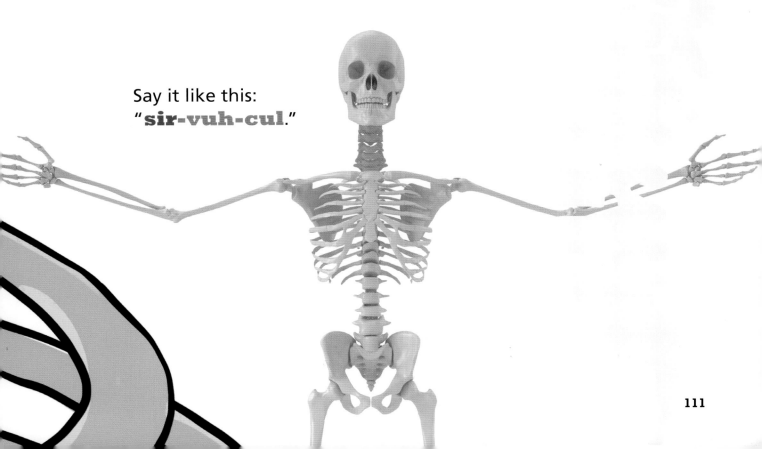

The Power in Posture

Did you know that standing and sitting up straight impacts how you feel? It's scientifically proven that maintaining good posture makes you feel better and also makes others feel good about you.

Remember, psychology follows physiology. What this means is that your state of mind is influenced by how your body is functioning and how well or poorly you're treating it.

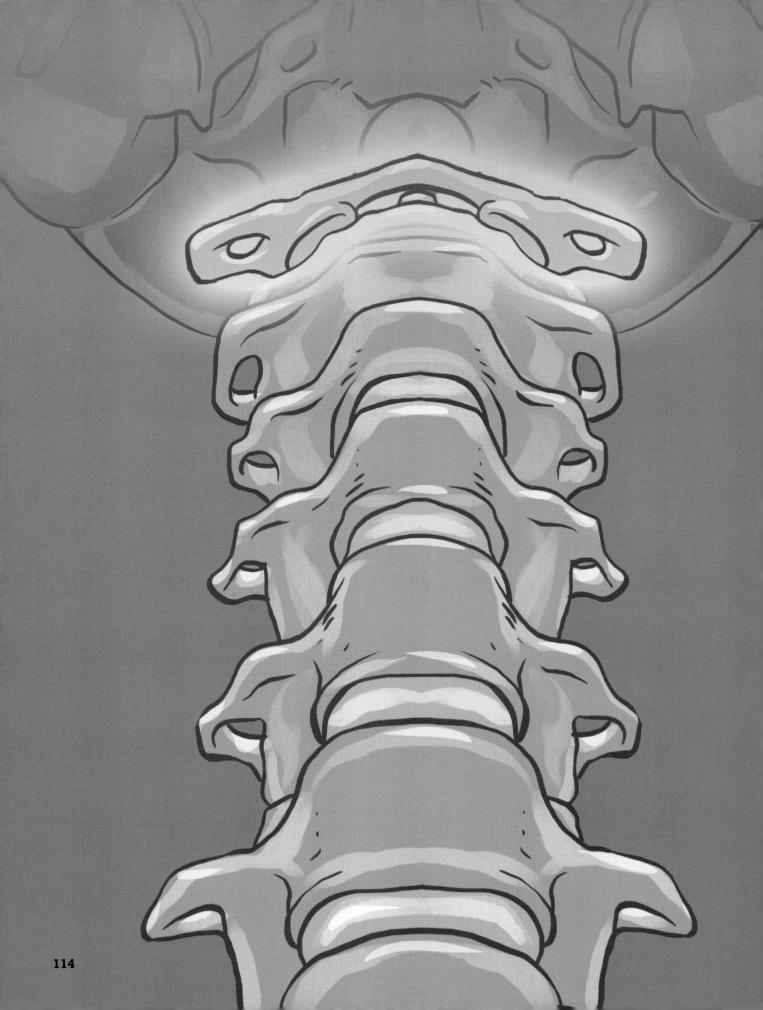

The Atlas

I know it might not be what you expected,
but *this* atlas gives you the best perspective.

In life, sometimes, we all get fed up,
but this bone helps you hold your head up.

And when you hold your head high, even if you're sad,
you tend to feel better, and a little bit more glad!

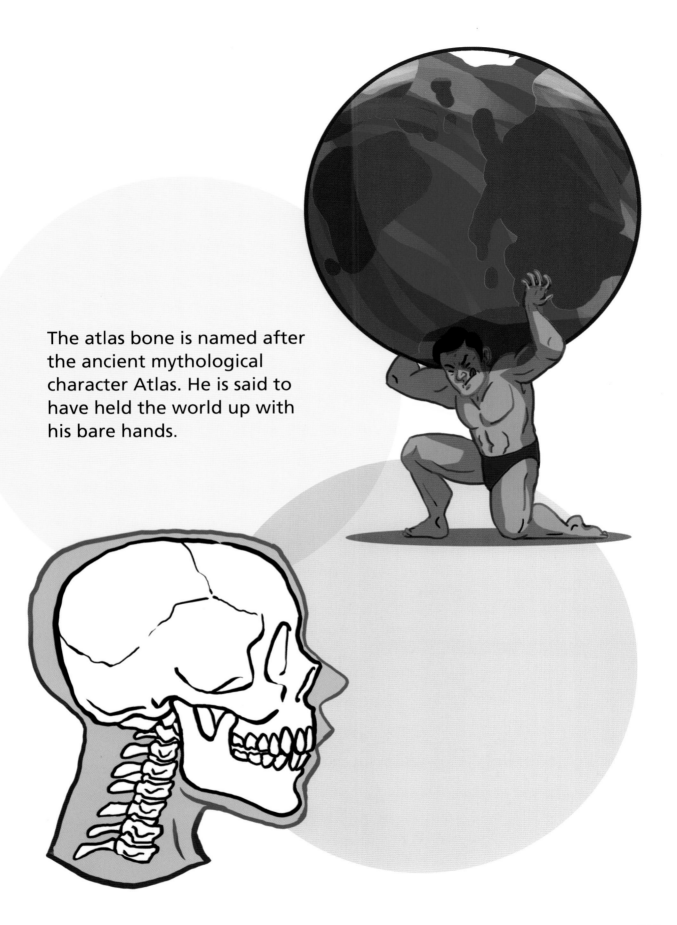

The atlas bone is named after the ancient mythological character Atlas. He is said to have held the world up with his bare hands.

The cervical section has seven vertebrae, C1 to C7.

These vertebrae are the smallest in the spine. They are smaller than those in the lumbar and thoracic sections because they have less weight to support.

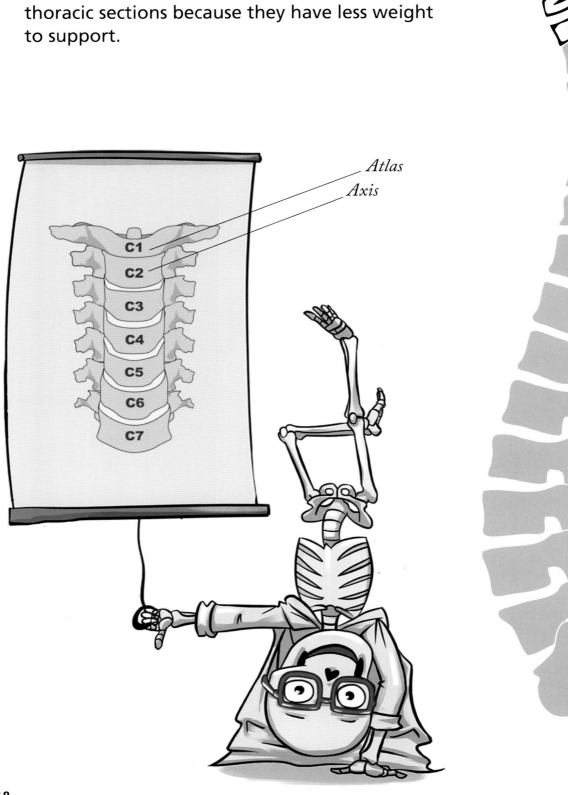

Atlas

Axis

C1
C2
C3
C4
C5
C6
C7

Cervical comes from the Latin word *cervic,* which means "neck."

So you can remember that the cervical spine serves and supports you.

The Axis

The cervical section
helps your neck move
to and fro.

To nod your head "yes,"
and shake your head "no."

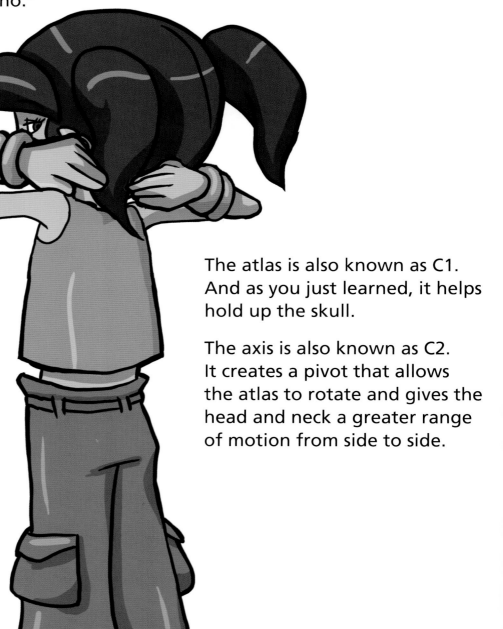

The atlas is also known as C1.
And as you just learned, it helps
hold up the skull.

The axis is also known as C2.
It creates a pivot that allows
the atlas to rotate and gives the
head and neck a greater range
of motion from side to side.

Special Cervicals

Most mammals have seven cervical vertebrae in their necks, except two extra-cuddly creatures: three-toed sloths (or is that three-phalanged sloths?) have eight or nine cervical vertebrae, and manatees have six.

Three-toed Sloth

Manatee (Sea Cow)

Amazingly, giraffes only
have seven cervical vertebrae…

 Human cervical vertebra

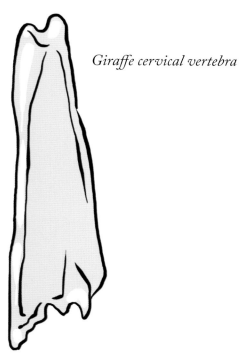

Giraffe cervical vertebra

…but each vertebra can be up to
10 inches long!

Take a look at how much bigger
a giraffe's cervical vertebra is
compared to a human's!

Rib Tickler *Did you know that the average length of a giraffe's neck is 6 feet?!*

Cervical Lordosis

Like the lumbar and thoracic sections of the spine, the cervical section also has a slight curve. It's called cervical lordosis.

Say it like this:
"sir-vuh-cul" — **"lor-doe-sis."**

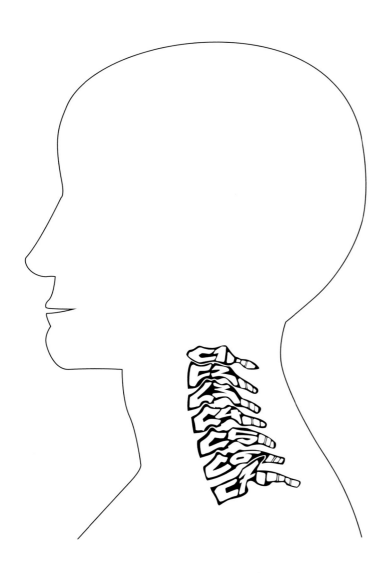

In a healthy spine,
the cervical lordosis looks like a banana.

Activity: Colors of the Spine

Front View

Color in the cervical section.

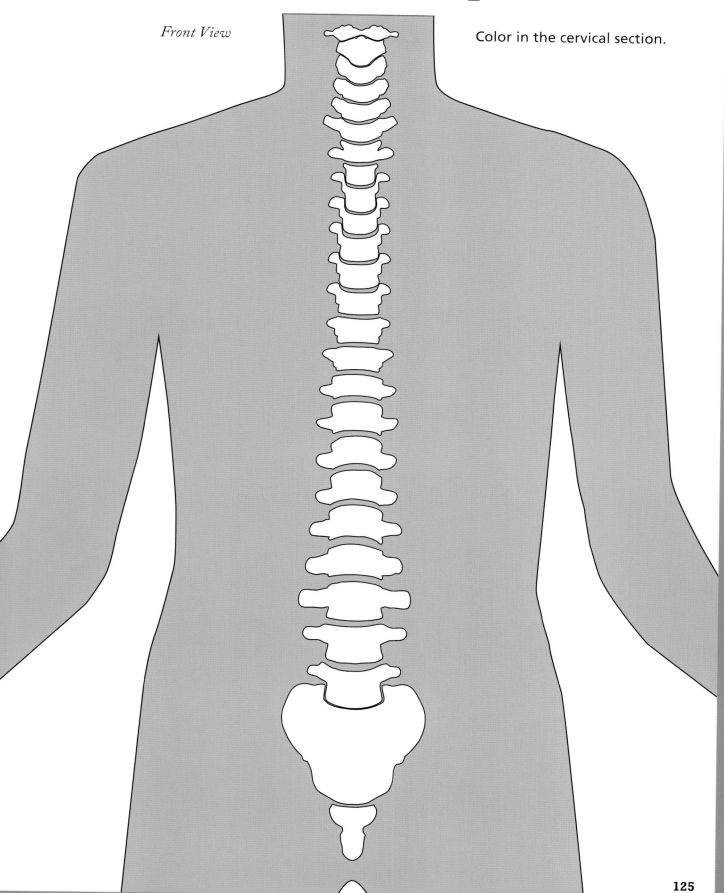

Text Neck

Keep your cervical section healthy! Many of us spend lots of time every day bending our necks down and staring at our smartphones or laptops. This poor posture, called text neck, can lead to early wear-and-tear on the spine, degeneration of the neck's natural curve, and even surgery.

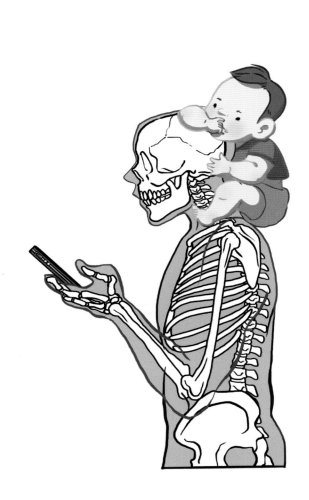

15 degree angle = 27 pounds

30 degree angle = 40 pounds

The average weight of our heads is 10 to 11 pounds. That's the natural weight that the cervical section is built to hold. Now imagine carrying the animals below on your neck. When you bend your head to text, you're actually putting that much weight on your cervical section. Ouch!

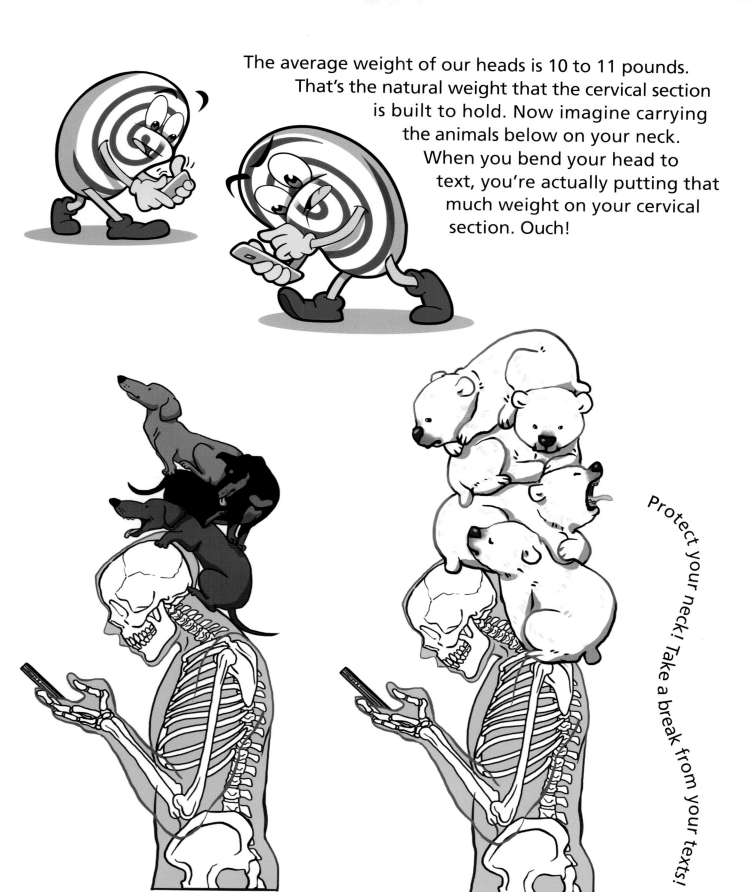

45 degree angle = 49 pounds

60 degree angle = 60 pounds

Protect your neck! Take a break from your texts!

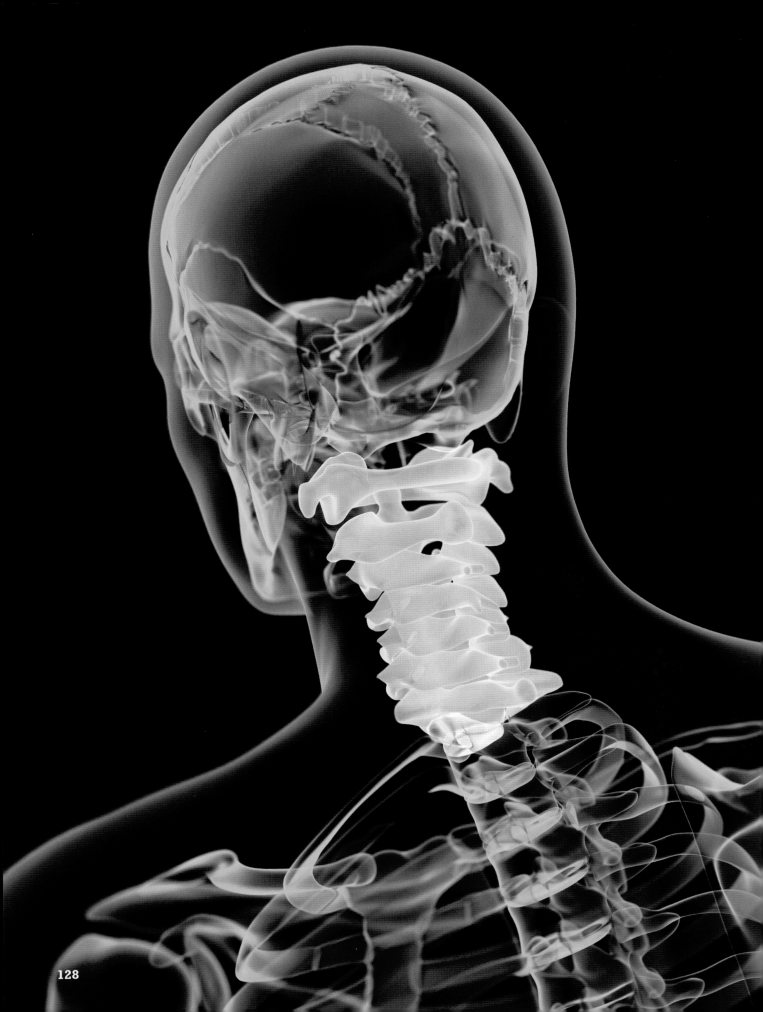

Now that you've gotten a sense of the entire cervical section, let's take a look at an individual vertebra. Here's how C4 looks from multiple angles.

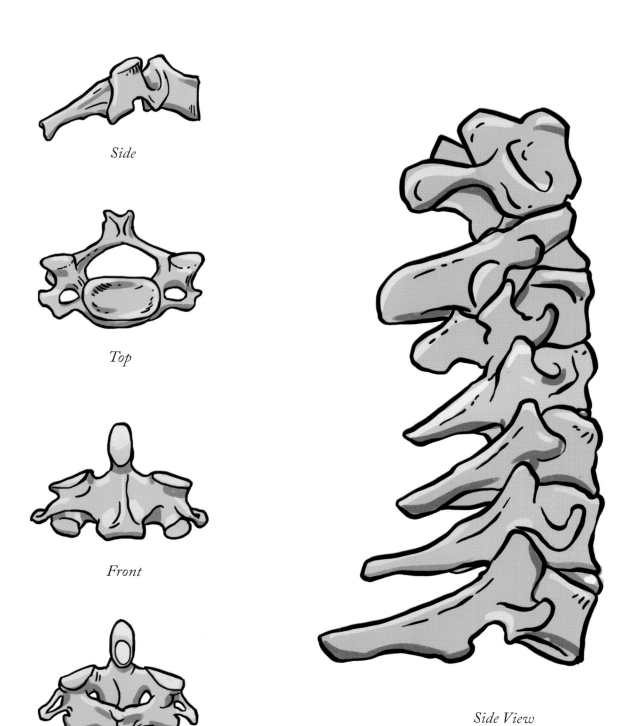

Side

Top

Front

Back

Side View

Activity: Cervical Slide

Put two fingers on each earlobe and slide them toward the back of your head until they rest in the soft spot in the middle of your skull, just above your neck. Now slide your fingers down the back of your neck until you come to the top of your back, where your shoulders begin. You might be able to feel some small bony bumps along the way— up and down the back of your neck. This is your cervical section.

Rib Tickler *Never lie to an X-ray technician. They can see right through you.*

Activity: Spine Match

Let's find out how much you remember about the lumbar, thoracic, and cervical sections. First, draw a line from the name of the spine section to the vertebra that corresponds with it. Then, draw another line from the vertebra to the area of the spine that it's located in.

Lumbar

Thoracic

Cervical

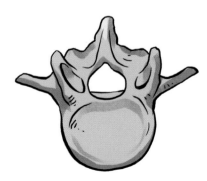

Top View

Side View

Crossword Bones
f the Spine and Rib Cage

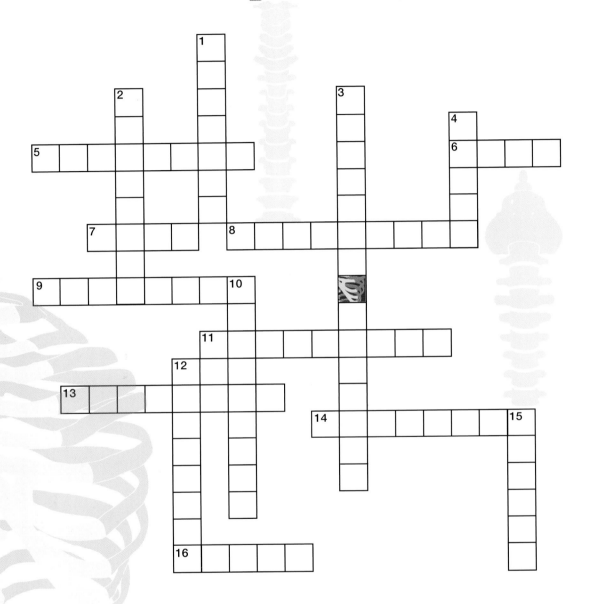

across

5. Which section of the spine has 12 vertebrae?

6. What is the name of the bone in the cervical section most responsible for the side-to-side rotation of the head?

7. How many lumbar vertebrae are there?

8. What connects the ribs to the sternum?

9. What are the two bottom ribs called?

11. What is the uppermost part of the sternum called?

13. What is the curve in the thoracic section called?

14. What is the uppermost section of the spine called?

16. What does the atlas hold up?

down

1. What is it called when your spine bends while you touch your toes?

2. What are the openings in the sacrum for nerves to travel through called?

3. What is the bottommost section of the sternum called?

4. What are ribs 8, 9, and 10 called?

10. What part of the sternum translates as "little sword"?

12. What is the curve in the lumbar and cervical sections called?

15. Which section of the spine has the largest and strongest vertebrae?

133

But before I tell you the one I came up with, why don't you create your own?

A mnemonic is a word-trick to help you remember the names of multiple things or places. We used them in Books 1 and 2 to help remember the bones of the hands and feet. Can you come up with a phrase that helps you remember the spine's five sections?

A mnemonic helps your memory. The "m" is silent. Say it like this: **"ne-mon-ick."**

Give it a shot:

C_____	S_____	L_____	T_____	C_____
O	A	U	H	E
C	C	M	O	R
C	R	B	R	V
Y	U	A	A	I
X	M	R	C	C
			I	A
			C	L

Turn the page to see how your mnemonic compares to Vinny's...

As you can see, these are no ordinary crickets.
Allow me to present them to you, and our mnemonic word-trick
to help you remember the five sections of the spine.

Crickets	**Sell**	**Litterboxes**	**To**	**Cats**
O	A	U	H	E
C	C	M	O	R
C	R	B	R	V
Y	U	A	A	I
X	M	R	C	C
			I	A
			C	L

Activity: Spine Review

Now you try it.

Write the names of each of the spine sections below.

Crickets Sell Litterboxes To Cats

---   ---   ---

---   ---   ---

---   ---   ---

---   ---   ---

---   ---   ---

139

Well, you already knew these were no ordinary crickets. But, my friends, these are no ordinary cats either.

Crickets **Sell** **Litterboxes** **To** **Real** **Smooth** **Cats**

Crickets	Sell	Litterboxes	To	Real	Smooth	Cats
O	A	U	H	I	T	E
C	C	M	O	B	E	R
C	R	B	R	S	R	V
Y	U	A	A		N	I
X	M	R	C		U	C
			I		M	A
			C			L

BONE-US MATH:

_____ bones in the spine

+ _____ ribs
(total number, not pairs)

+ _____ bone that protects the front of the body

= _____ bones in the spine and rib cage

That's a lot of bones!

141

We Did It!

Well done, Bonyfide Buddies!
What dedication you've shown.
You're a spine and rib cage expert,
and your mind, it has grown.

You've learned 51 bones
of the structure inside.
Your knowledge has power.
CONGRATS, you're Bonyfide!

Wait! Before you head out,
there's more knowledge to gain.
It's some fun Bone-Us Knowledge
to tickle your brain.

And you've earned one more surprise.
Check the back of this book.
It's your official certificate.
Go on, take a look!

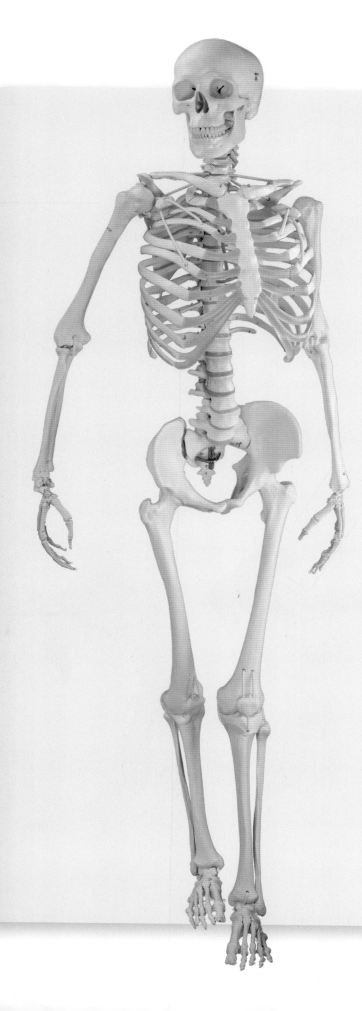

Know Yourself Academy's
Bone-Us Knowledge

Now that you've learned the bones of the rib cage and spine, step right up for some **Bone-Us Knowledge**! These pages will help you understand your body even more.

143

Spinal Motion

The spine is the most central skeletal structure in the human body. It is what provides the main support for your body, allowing you to stand upright, bend, and twist. The spine has four primary movements: flexion (bending forward), extension (bending back), rotation (turning side to side), and lateral flexion (bending side to side).

The primary motions in the lumbar section are flexion and extension. The primary motion in the thoracic section is rotation, because that's how the rib cage moves. The majority of cervical section rotation happens in the upper cervical between the atlas and the axis.

Flexion   Extension   Rotation   Lateral Flexion

Proper Standing Posture

Posture is the way you hold your body. Having good posture helps you stay healthy and also feel good about yourself. It is a practice that is developed in the same way as brushing your teeth or washing your hands. It is easier to learn proper posture when you are young. Proper posture will help you avoid spinal distortion, nerve damage, and the resulting symptoms of back pain, muscle tension, and problems with joints, bones, and organs.

The spine has curves to support a lifetime of standing, sitting, walking, and running. The spine also carries the body's components, such as the heavy skull, which protects the brain, and the nervous system, which controls all body functions. Preserving the spinal curves is essential to maximum health and function of the body.

Proper standing posture looks like this:

- The ears, shoulders, knees, and ankles are all lined up.
- Stand with your weight on the balls of your feet (not with weight on your heels).
- Keep your knees soft (don't lock them).
- Tuck your chin a bit.
- If you are standing for a long time, you can rock slightly heel to toe or shift weight from one foot to the other.

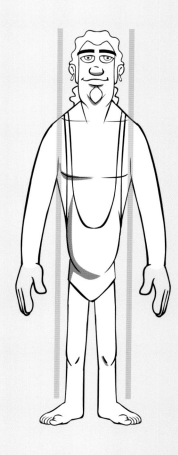

Proper Sitting or Moving Posture

Have you ever seen a lion walking in the desert with its chest up, open and proud? Well this is exactly how human spines were designed to be positioned. What we often forget is that every action we do influences the shape of our spine. When we slouch on the couch, our spine loses its original shape and changes the amount of blood passing through the body, which makes us feel tired. When we run, our spine gains strength, helping our body to work at its best.

The manubrium of the sternum should be your compass for proper posture. When the sternum is lifted, posture is improved; when the sternum is dropped, posture is poor. If you remember to lead with your heart, your body will carry you far.

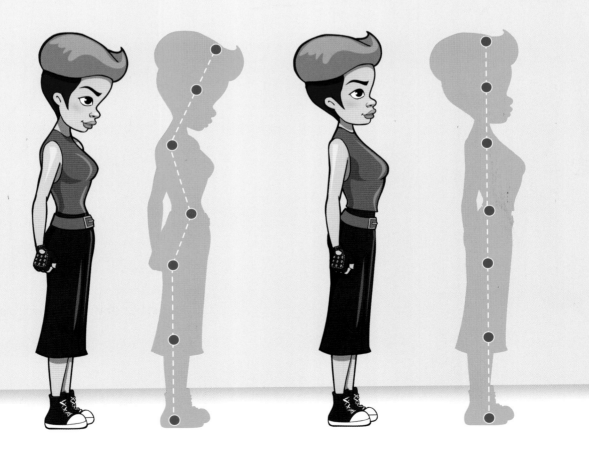

Proper Sleeping Posture

Have you ever fallen asleep while sitting up?
Have you ever dozed off while watching television, reading a book, or riding in a car?

Those who are able to fall asleep while sitting often wake up feeling drowsy and with muscle aches. This is because your spine is in an uncomfortable and unnatural position for sleep when sitting.

Your posture while sleeping is important for spinal health in the same way that proper posture is important while standing, sitting, or moving. Sleeping properly will help prevent problems with your bones, joints, muscles, and nerves, and will help you wake up feeling more refreshed and energized.

Try to avoid sleeping on your stomach, since that flattens the natural curve of the spine, which can lead to lower back pain.

If you sleep on your back, use one pillow that supports your neck. A pillow under your knees will reduce pressure on your lower spine.

If you sleep on your side, use a pillow to keep your head and neck level. Bend at your hips and knees, but don't curl up into a ball.

Ribs in Relationship

All by themselves the ribs are quite strong. They are stiff and solid, and that's what makes them great at protecting our most important organs, like the heart, the lungs, the liver, the gallbladder, and the kidneys.

But it's when the ribs work in relationship with the muscles and the organs around them that they truly serve their purpose.

Just think, you may be really smart and really strong, but when you work in relationship with your friends and your family, you can be even more effective at whatever you're doing!

Ribs in Relationship:
Intercostal Muscles (Part 1)

Remember when you gave yourself a rib wrap?
The place your hands landed is also called the thoracic wall.

The thoracic wall is made up of all 12 pairs of ribs and the intercostal muscles that connect each rib to the one above it and the one below it.

Say it like this: "*in-ter-**cobs**-taal.*"

Without these connective muscles, ribs would be a stiff ladder of bones. They would have no ability to move up or down, in or out, and you could only take one size of breath!

When the ribs are connected by the intercostal muscles, the muscles stretch in and out, up and down, taking the ribs with them to make room for air to enter and exit the lungs.

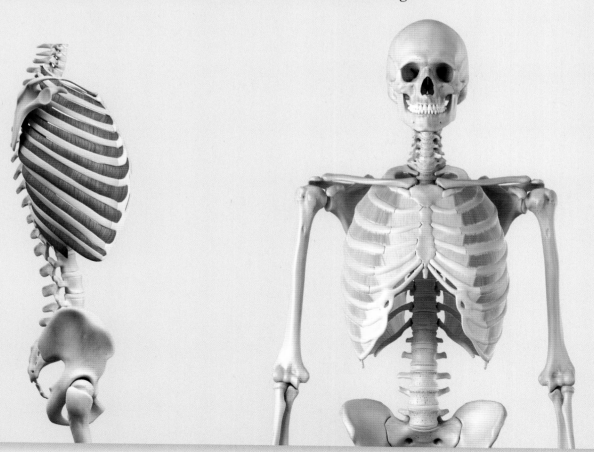

Ribs in Relationship: Intercostal Muscles (Part 2)

How exactly do the intercostal muscles move the ribs? Is it up or down? Or in and out?

It's both!

Think of a bucket (a beach bucket, a water pail, or anything with a handle). Now imagine the handle rising a bit and falling a bit, as if you were picking it up and dropping it.

When you inhale, the intercostal muscles contract (pull together) and the bucket handle goes up. This is what makes the rib cage rise.

When you exhale, the intercostal muscles expand (release) and the bucket handle falls. This is what makes the rib cage drop.

The same is true of the sternum. Imagine it like the handle of a water pump. When you inhale, the intercostal muscles push the sternum forward. When you exhale, the intercostal muscles pull the sternum in.

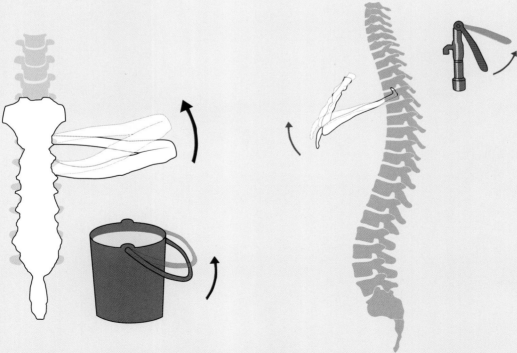

Ribs in Relationship: Diaphragm

Say it like this: *"die-uh-fram."*

The diaphragm is a muscle very important to breathing. It is located just beneath rib 6, right around the tip of the xiphoid process, and goes all the way down to rib 10. Without this muscle, we couldn't take the deep inhales and exhales we need to lift weights, swim under water, or yell "Goaaaaaal!!!" Do you want to see yours in action?

Find a ball (any old ball will do). Lie down on your back. Use your hands to find the spot where we located the end of the sternum, where the ribs no longer touch in the middle. Do you feel that hollow? Now place the ball there. Carefully balance the ball until it is still. When you've got it sitting on top of you like a bump on a log, take a deep breath in.

The ball rolls off!

Why? Because the diaphragm muscle is moving! It is dropping farther down the thoracic wall to make room for the lungs to expand. When you breathe out, the diaphragm moves back up into the chest cavity.

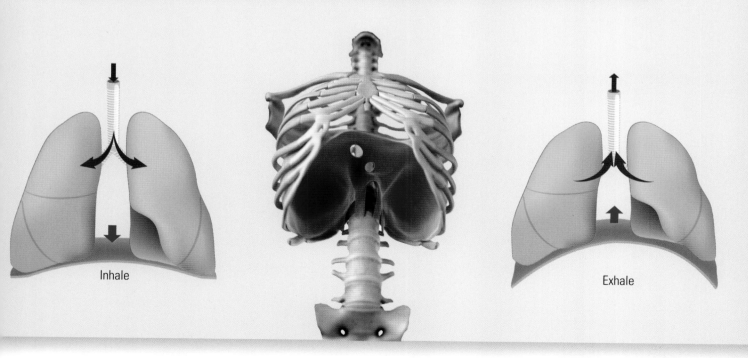

Inhale

Exhale

Curious Cuneiform Code

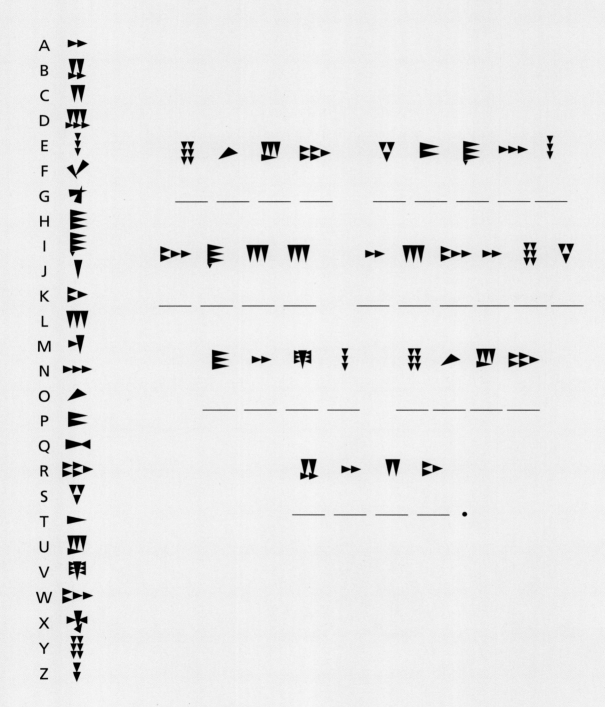

Bone-Us Quiz

1. Which section of the spine has flexion and extension as its primary motion? _____

2. What is the primary motion of the thoracic section of the spine?
    A) rotation
    B) flexion
    C) lateral flexion
    D) extension

3. Which of the following is NOT proper standing posture?
    A) knees soft (not locked)
    B) standing with your weight on your heels
    C) ears, shoulders, knees, and ankles lined up

4. Why is proper posture important for human beings? _____

5. True or False? When the sternum is lifted, posture is improved. _____

6. Is it possible for your spine to lose its original shape? _____

7. True or False? Your posture while sleeping is just as important for spinal health as your posture when standing. _____

8. Name two of the vital organs that the rib cage protects. _____

9. True or False? The thoracic wall is made up of 10 pairs of ribs. _____

10. Name one important function of the diaphragm. _____

Answer Key

Page 16

Page 25

Any of the following answers are acceptable:

It helps us balance when sitting.

It is shaped like a beak.

Its name derives from the Greek word kokkux.

It begins as three to five soft, separate bones, and as we get older, ossifies into a single, hard bone.

Page 40

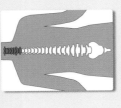

Page 50

Page 57

Page 69

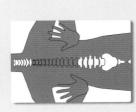

Page 91

Name the three different parts that make up the rib cage.

Ribs, sternum, and vertebrae.

How many pairs of ribs does the human body contain?

12

What are the names of the three different types of ribs?

True ribs, false ribs, and floating ribs.

Name one of the main functions of the ribs.

They help protect our vital organs, such as the heart and lungs.

Which vertebra does rib 7 connect to?

T7

What is cartilage?

Cartilage is a strong but flexible material found in some parts of the body. It provides support without being as hard or rigid as bone.

There are seven pairs of true ribs.

There are three pairs of false ribs.

There are two pairs of floating ribs.

Page 94

Page 103

Why not just walk across rib 1, which links up to T1?

Page 106

Page 125

Page 131

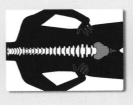

Page 132

Page 138

Crickets Sell Litterboxes To Cats

```
o   a   u   h   e
c   c   m   o   r
c   r   b   r   v
y   u   a   a   i
x   m   r   c   c
        i   a
        c   l
```

Page 141

26 bones in the spine

24 ribs

1 bone that protects the front of the body

51 bones in the spine and rib cage

Page 152

Y O U R   S P I N E

W I L L   A L W A Y S

H A V E   Y O U R

B A C K .

Page 153

1. Lumbar section
2. A) rotation
3. B) standing with your weight on your heels
4. Proper posture enables lifelong health.
5. True
6. Yes (but exercise and good posture can prevent this from happening).
7. True
8. Heart, lungs, liver, gallbladder, kidneys
9. False, the thoracic wall is made up of 12 pairs of ribs.
10. Breathing

Glossary

Atlas: The topmost bone in the spinal column, also called C1. It is located in the cervical section of the spine. It is the bone responsible for holding up the head. Because of this, it is named after the ancient mythological character Atlas, who is said to have held the world up with his bare hands.

Axis: The second topmost bone in the spinal column, also called C2. It is located in the cervical section of the spine. It is the bone that creates a pivot allowing the atlas, or C1, to rotate. It is largely responsible for the side-to-side movement of the head.

Boneology: The study of bones with Dr. Bonyfide. When you study bones in medical school it is called osteology.

Bones: Any of the pieces of hard, connective tissue making up the skeletal framework in humans and other vertebrates. Without bones, our bodies would be like jelly.

Cartilage: A strong but flexible material found in some parts of the body. It provides support without being as hard or rigid as bone. It connects the ribs to the sternum. Because it is so flexible, it helps the rib cage expand.

Cervical: The section of the spine found between the top of the neck and the top of the shoulders. The cervical section is composed of seven vertebrae, which are the smallest in the spine. These vertebrae, particularly the atlas and the axis, are responsible for movement of the head.

Cervical Lordosis: The natural inward curve of the cervical section. In a healthy spine, the cervical lordosis looks like a banana.

Coccyx: The lowest bone of the spinal column, commonly known as the tailbone.

Etymology: The study of the history of words and how they change over time.

Extension: When your spine lengthens and your chest moves outward, as you bend backward.

False Ribs: Ribs 8, 9, and 10 are called false ribs because they do not connect to the sternum with their own piece of cartilage. They reach up and attach to the cartilage of rib 7.

Flexion: When your spine arches while you touch your toes, as you bend forward.

Floating Ribs: Ribs 11 and 12 are called floating ribs because they do not attach to the sternum or to cartilage. They start at the 11th and 12th thoracic vertebrae and simply end in the middle of our bodies, just above the outside of our hip bones.

Foramina: The holes that line both sides of the sacrum. These openings are for nerves to travel through.

Gladiolus: The middle section of the sternum.

Invertebrate: A living organism that does not have a spine. Jellyfish, sea anemones, spiders, octopuses, and snails are examples of invertebrates.

Lateral Flexion: When your spine stretches while you tilt from side to side.

Lumbar: The section of the spine found between the pelvis and the rib cage. The lumbar section is comprised of five vertebrae, which are the largest and the strongest in the spine. These vertebrae are thick and sturdy to support the weight of the body.

Lumbar Lordosis: The natural inward curve of the spine's lumbar section.

Manubrium: The uppermost section of the sternum.

Mnemonic: A learning tool such as an acronym, rhyme, or song to help us remember information. Crickets Sell Litterboxes To Real Smooth Cats is an example.

Nerve: A fiber or bundle of fibers that transmits impulses of sensation to the brain or spinal cord, and impulses from these to the muscles and organs.

Organism: Literally, a "living thing." The word organism comes from the Greek words organon, meaning "body organ," and ismos, meaning "system."

Ossification: The hardening of cartilage or muscular tissue into bone. When a baby is born, some of their "bones" are actually soft cartilage, which allows for growth. As the child grows, these soft areas ossify into actual bone.

Osteologist: A doctor who specializes in osteology.

Glossary (continued)

Osteology: The branch of anatomy that deals with the structure and function of bones. When you study bones with Dr. Bonyfide, it is called boneology.

Psychology: The scientific study of the human mind and its functions, especially those affecting behavior.

Physiology: The scientific study of living organisms and the normal functions of their bodies.

Rib Cage: The structure made of bone and cartilage that makes up a core structure of the human skeleton, enclosing the heart, lungs, and other vital organs. It is formed of the sternum, the 12 thoracic vertebrae, and the 12 pairs of ribs connected to those vertebrae.

Ribs: The 12 pairs of arched bones that form the skeletal structure of the chest. There are three types of ribs: true ribs, false ribs, and floating ribs.

Sacrum: The large, anchor-shaped bone at the base of the spine. It forms the solid base of the spinal column, connecting to the coccyx on the bottom, and the lumbar section on top. The sacrum forms the posterior, or backside, of the pelvis. Along with the hips, the sacrum helps to carry the body's weight.

Skeleton: The 206 bones that form the framework of the adult human body.

Spinal Cord: The bundle of nerve fibers and tissue, housed by the spine, that carries messages between the brain and the rest of the body.

Spine: The strong and flexible structure of vertebrae extending from the skull to the small of the back that provides support for the human body and protects the spinal cord. The spine is also referred to as the spinal column and the backbone.

Sternum: The long, sword-shaped bone located in the center of the chest, along the midline of the body.

Text Neck: Poor posture created by bending our necks down and staring at our smartphones or laptops. It can lead to early wear-and-tear on the spine, degeneration of the neck's natural curve, and even surgery.

Thoracic: The longest section of the spine, found in the middle and upper part of the back. The thoracic section is made up of 12 vertebrae, which are intermediate in size between the cervical and lumbar vertebrae. Each of the thoracic section's 12 vertebrae connects to an individual rib.

Thoracic Kyphosis: The natural outward curve of the spine's thoracic section.

Tissue: Any of the distinct types of material animals or plants are made of.

True Ribs: Ribs 1 through 7 are true ribs. The true ribs start just beneath the collarbone and end in the middle of the torso. They are called true ribs because they all have their own strip of cartilage that connects them to the sternum.

Vertebra: Any of the small bones that make up the spine.

Vertebrae: The plural form of vertebra. There are 26 total vertebrae in the spinal column.

Vertebrate: A living organism that has a spine. Mammals, reptiles, amphibians, birds, and fish are examples of vertebrates.

Xiphoid Process: The bottommost section of the sternum. It is a soft, pointy piece of cartilage that takes up to 40 years before it hardens completely into bone.

Contributors

Managing Editor
Ed Ntiri

Story Editor
Raphael Cohen

Art Director
Erik Ramirez

Visual Designer
Breena Nuñez

Writers
Patrick Castrenze

Laleh Khadivi

Publishing Consultant
Derek Bacchus

Writing and Research Credits
Linda A. Balfour

Raphael Cohen

Dr. Ben Glass

Lidie Howes

Nancy Howes

Dr. Timothy Howes

Ed Ntiri

Bonnie O'Connell

Dr. Matt Rivera

Kimberly Stinson Serrano

Joanie Thompson

Illustration Credits
Chris Fenoglio

Leonardo Gonzalez

Barbara Kalustian

Rachel Ann Millar

Breena Nuñez

Jovan Obradovic

Erik Ramirez

Milena Salieri

Roni Setiawan

Shutterstock.com

Notes

In this 12-part adventure, you will learn about your body from the inside out. You will embark on a time-traveling expedition with Dr. Bonyfide, where you will encounter historical figures that serve to teach important lessons about how the body works, while also getting into some mischief along the way.

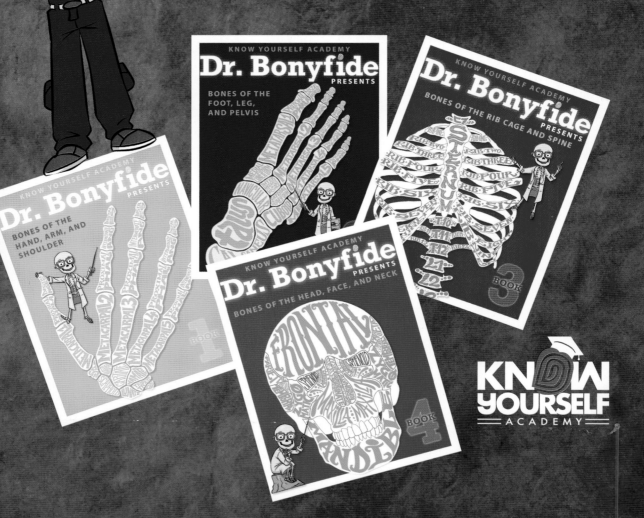